What people are saying about *Rawumptious Recipes:*

"By including her journey toward a living food diet, June connects the dots for us. Through her everyday 'mom-ness' somehow the mystery of a raw foods lifestyle falls away to a greater appreciation and understanding of this ultimate approach to healthy choices geared toward families with children."

Anna Anawalt
Friend, Neighbor and Mom

"Thank you for writing this book, June. Thanks for pointing out how easy it can be to feed children and families amazingly healthy foods. Thanks for putting together the science *and* common sense, which should convince even doctors that our children deserve far better food than what we, as parents, are feeding them. I love watching your family eat and live this way, and you inspire me, too."

Jay Gordon, MD, FAAP, IBCLC, FABM
Associate Professor of Pediatrics, UCLA School of Medicine
Former Senior Fellow in Pediatric Nutrition, Memorial Sloan-Kettering Institute, co-author of *The ADD and ADHD Cure: The Natural Way to Treat Hyperactivity and Refocus Your Child*

"As a family therapist whose clientele includes many children with the ADHD label, I've seen the undeniable benefits of feeding them whole, natural foods. What makes June Louks's book so remarkable is that her recipes are the epitome of 'good for you' eating, yet are tasty enough to appeal to even picky eaters. When children are fueled by the kinds of healthy dishes June has put together, they literally have the raw ingredients to help them better manage their behavior, mood and focus. *Rawupmtious Recipes* is a winner!"

Susan Stiffelman, MFT, author of *Cool, Calm and Connected: Raising Joyful, Resilient Kids without Power Struggles, Arguments and Meltdowns*

"I'm re-reading the manuscript. I must say it is so well done and it makes me teary eyed. It is very inspiring to read, knowing your joy to be writing and sharing the gift of God's Love as it so flowed through the written word, your words flow with Living Waters, shining the Light of Truth page after page. Thank you for doing all you do. You are God's love in action. Blessings"

Don Kidson
Friend and Mentor

"Thank you for taking the time to show us the light! Your insight into developing the lifestyles not only for us, but also our children, is perfect. Your passion is very inspiring. The detailed tools, suggestions and recipes are easy to follow and apply to our everyday lives. Taking your suggestions to supply fresh fruit, raw veggies, etc., as a number-one option to our kids was actually a big hit. We are now establishing healthy food choice foundations that will hopefully be our framework for life.

We think *Rawumptious* should have a place in every home and school."
The Shelby Family

"As a busy vegetarian mom, I'm always on the lookout for nutritious meals that are easy to prepare. June Louks has put together an entire book's worth! And with these Rawumptious Recipes you'll never have to say, "Just eat it anyway. It's good for you," because these recipes are kid-approved!

Martha Quinn
Sirius/XM Radio Host

Rawumptious Recipes

A Family's Adventure to Healthy, Happy, and Harmonious Living

By the Louks Family: June, Jeff, Lauren, Heather, Hailey, and Charlotte Louks

iUniverse, Inc.
New York   Bloomington

Rawumptious Recipes
A Family's Adventure to Healthy, Happy, Harmonious Living

The statements in this book have not been evaluated by the Food and Drug Administration (FDA) and are not intended to be a substitute for medical advice. Please supervise young children while eating all foods, especially hard foods.

iUniverse books may be ordered through booksellers or by contacting:

iUniverse
1663 Liberty Drive
Bloomington, IN 47403
www.iuniverse.com
1-800-Authors (1-800-288-4677)

Because of the dynamic nature of the Internet, any Web addresses or links contained in this book may have changed since publication and may no longer be valid. The views expressed in this work are solely those of the author and do not necessarily reflect the views of the publisher, and the publisher hereby disclaims any responsibility for them.

ISBN: 978-1-4401-2525-6 (sc)
ISBN: 978-1-4401-2526-3 (ebook)

Printed in the United States of America

iUniverse rev. date: 04/03/2009

This book is dedicated to Don Kidson. Thank you, Don, for giving us those books, compact disk, and DVD, even though they sat in a drawer for a long time. Thank you for your vision and gentle yet consistent encouragement. You inspire us with your willingness to let go of self and follow your inner leadings so that something much more profound and healing for mankind and our planet can come forth.

Contents

About the Authors

Jeff and June Louks have been married for twenty years and have dated since their teens. (And they are still crazy about each other!) Although their oldest daughters, Lauren and Heather, are twins from birth, their youngest, Charlotte and Hailey, are twins in spirit.

A little about each family member:

    Lauren: age twelve, ranked tennis player and honor student
    Heather: age twelve, accomplished gymnast and straight-A student
    Hailey: age nine, actress/entertainer
    Charlotte: age six, homeschooling love child
    June: surfer, nurturer, homemaker, educator, garden enthusiast and architect
    Jeff: breadwinner, surfer, involved dad, supportive husband

The family often enjoys going to the Malibu beach and surfing together as a family. They eat breakfast and dinner together every day.

Preface

This book offers support, insight, information, and inspiration for families and individuals who want to move toward mouthwatering, yet sustainable (nonimpact), foods that are living (or full of life, with no raw yet dead meat and minimal processing); a delicious plant-based diet you and your family will love. It is not intended to promote a rigid diet with a strict set of rules. It is an offering for those who choose to move out of the current hogwash of highly processed, denatured foods that are eroding our health. It is an offering to support you in moving toward selecting energizing, cleansing foods that also contribute to healing our planet.

This book might encourage you to make minor lifestyle adjustments, like choosing an organic apple over a candy bar for your next snack. Or, you might choose to have a raw family meal once a week. As Americans, how would we impact our world and our health if plants became our main course and the other food was served on the side? Whether you and your family aim for 10 percent, 50 percent, or even 80 percent whole foods, moving in this direction can be an exhilarating, fulfilling, bonding journey that will send out ripples of blessing to humanity, our planet, and our children.

You might be a vegetarian already. In that case, you are already far along the path of nonimpacting our world, and you may be farther along on the road to whole foods, as well. Our family was not vegetarian or vegan when we first began our path a few years ago. In fact, we were skeptical of these practices because the vegetarians we knew were often low energy, pale faced, or even dealing with mental illness (no kidding). To be fair, some of these people were junk-food vegetarians who avoided meat and instead filled up on sourdough bread, pasta, and an extra helping of dessert. Still, we wondered if they were missing something. On the other hand, the several raw foodists we had met impressed us with their level of health, vitality, and glow. They were living transparencies for good, accomplishing what many would deem impossible.

I began my journey curious to know their secret but also very cautious because I didn't want my beloved family to fall into the pitfalls we had seen with some vegetarians and vegans. We also needed a fresh alternative to encouraging our kids to eat their (often soggy, overcooked) veggies. In the following pages, we share with you the results of our in-depth study and research, and the path we forged as a family toward a new approach to food.

With the fast-paced movement most busy families are experiencing nowadays, food quality often moves to the bottom on the list of priorities. We pull up to the drive-thru to fuel up our bellies as we do our cars. When we start to take ownership and accept responsibility for the ripples we're sending out, and when we see food as a beautiful offering—a divine communication from the source of all life—food begins to take a more important place in our lives.

June Louks

Testimonials

Rawumptious Recipes is truly the embodiment of pure goodness! June Louks introduced to me the healing qualities of living foods. As a medical doctor with over thirty years of practice, and a specialty in Emergency Medicine, I have seen my share of illness, disorders, disease and trauma. However, having enjoyed excellent health all my life until about five years ago, treating others did not prepare me for my own battle with ill health. Medically uncontrolled Type II Diabetes Mellitus, and a debilitating gastrointestinal bleed requiring blood transfusions, finally awakened me to the seriousness of my condition. With June's help and guidance, and the loving and caring support of my wife, Deborah, I was introduced to the healing nature of a living diet. June's recipes and expert preparations assisted my transformation towards a live raw food lifestyle, where foods that are lovingly grown, harvested and prepared can give the body the nutrition necessary to allow the body to reach its maximum health potential. These are foods and dishes that not only *look good*, they *taste unbelievably good*, and are *nothing but good for you*! The living raw food diet allows one to eat as much as one wishes, assuring you never feel hungry, and automatically re-adjusts the body's metabolism, bringing one's weight back into a more natural balance. My own weight dropped over fifty pounds in just over two months (246 to 195 at 6'2"). Decades-long joint pains all but vanished, and half a dozen formerly mandatory medications were stopped. Weight lost, energy gained, pains and fatigue banished, all achieved without the gnawing hunger usually associated with dieting. The living, raw food diet isn't a "diet" but rather a return to a more natural way of caring for one's body, allowing it to find and create balance without having to waste energy detoxifying the multitude of pollutants associated with the modern highly processed diet. Anyone wishing to have a more energy-filled, productive life need only to turn to the pages of June Loukses book and put into practice the natural healing capacity of the information and recipes contained inside.

Steven P. Grahek, MD, FAAEM

We have known the Louks family for just a year and thought their food protocols were interesting, challenging *but* not for us. God is great and had another plan ... my husband's diabetes and sudden health crisis last summer caused me to want, actually need, to learn more. And *wow*, what a journey. I never would have believed it was possible to witness and experience such results so fast. Simply by feeding the system real nourishment rather than fooling the system with food that filled, but did not feed us, I learned to appreciate and value the difference immediately. One does not need to eat as much or as often. I feel satisfied, energized, and inspired in ways I never imagined were possible.

Also, in spite of a family and personal history of *very* high cholesterol, I have been resisting taking cholesterol-lowering medicine for more than a year. After a month on a low glycemic (low sugar) live raw foods diet my cholesterol is down over one hundred points! I exercise a little but not nearly as much as I thought would be necessary to result in this level of change. *It is the diet and a shift in attitude from resigned to resilient! I am so grateful for life, hope and this inspiring family friendship—it is such a gift.* Our daughter was rarely willing to eat vegetables or salad greens until modeled by the Louks girls. After hanging out with them, she now she can enjoy a salad and is much more open to trying new foods. Thank you, June, Jeff, Olga, and all the girls for your persistence, love, and constant support. You have given us a new lease on life—indeed you have given us back our life!

Deborah La Gorce Kramer (Grahek)

Hi June:

I hope all is well with you. Ever since we read your book, my wife Nancy has made an unbelievable effort to get us all back on track to eating raw. Also, slowly but surely, she been ridding the house of the processed, cooked foods and replacing the free space with items that can be nutritionally described as, well, *food*. She's had our dehydrator on, almost nonstop, for the past couple of weeks and placed it in a position of prominence on our kitchen counter. She's pulled out the trusty old sprouting jars and put them back into active service. She's also spent an enormous amount of time reading various new raw-food books and re-reading some of the books that I purchased and read during my 100 percent raw-food days. Needless to say, I am very impressed with her level of commitment, especially given that the kids are still putting up some resistance.

Several of your recipes have been *very well received* by Nancy and the kids. For me, since I have long found pleasure in exploring prepared raw food meals, these recipes have really been a big treat. So, once again, I want to thank you so much for bringing the spark of responsible eating back to my wife and me and the critters (my kids).

Joseph R. Berkson
Senior Investment Associate

June's informative yet simple to understand book has literally contributed to changing my life. After gaining extra pounds during my middle aged years, it gave me the simple ABC's of getting rid of the extra weight. Her delightful samples to me and our class were just the thing to entice me into a new life of integrating the live foods into my diet I so desperately needed. I have trimmed down to a healthy weight and feel new vitality! (I've lost twenty-five pounds eating good food and exercising.) Thanks, June!

Ms. Walton, Teacher, CCS

June! Since your girls changed their diets (and avoided processed sugars and flours), their plaque levels are down and they no longer are getting cavities! What a difference their diet has made! The typical American diet is not good for our children's teeth. I want all my clients to know about your book and the healthy, yummy alternatives it offers!

Dr. Lynn Watenabe, DDS
The Dental Spa

Our family of five had the pleasure of spending an entire month with the Louks family at their home. Their life in Malibu is truly spectacular. They have created a clean, healthy and active lifestyle for their family of six. I hadn't seen my dear friend June for two and a half years when we paid this extended visit. I was struck by how incredibly stunning and fit she looked. In fact, her entire family looked amazing. I found out quickly that they had shifted to a profoundly healthful and natural lifestyle. From the moment I walked through the front door of their home, I knew there was something extra special about their life. Even the smell of their home is unique. It has an unbelievably fresh scent. It literally smells like a garden of vegetables, fruits and herbs. There are no lingering smells of heavy cleansers, or cooked foods that could attach to your clothes. The kitchen countertops have large bowls and platters that are stuffed with fresh fruits. The children happily help themselves throughout the day to these healthy choices. The pantry is a place you want to explore. It is meticulously organized with dried fruit, bulk grains, beans and organic pastas. Glass containers are filled to the brim with June's homemade, dehydrated raw crackers and granola, both of which are my personal favorites. I loved helping myself throughout the day to these healthy choices!

June taught me how to begin each day with a raw, green smoothie. This sets the tone for a day full of energy and stamina. A truly magical time at the Louks home is dinnertime. The entire family gathers at a long dining table where June serves raw and mostly vegan meals that she has seamlessly organized and prepared. Her children often help June gather the fresh vegetables, greens and fruits, from their backyard garden, that she uses in her meals. These meals are satisfying and bountiful and usually include a scrumptious raw desert! I was amazed the first night we joined them for dinner. June had a selection of lasagna for our large group. There was organic, cooked lasagna for her guests, along with her raw lasagna. Being a raw skeptic at the time, I was convinced that I would only enjoy the cooked lasagna. I was wrong. The raw lasagna won the taste test by a landslide. It was incredible! It had layers of fresh vegetables and herbs with a delicious pine nut sauce. I had never tasted anything like it and my children responded enthusiastically. It was quite an experience. As our families enjoyed our first raw meal together, we talked with June and Jeff about their raw 'alkaline' lifestyle and their philosophies. They emphasized the importance of thinking outside of the mainstream influences that popular culture and the media tries to sell to us. After dinner we danced for hours to the children's favorite songs, which is also part of the Louks lifestyle. We felt satiated from our meal, yet light and healthy. As I danced I looked around at the joy being expressed by all. I remember thinking that there is a serenity in the Louks home that their raw lifestyle enhances. I knew that they are really on to something special.

What an inspiration is was to spend a month with this family. My family has gone from eating a "mainstream" diet, to really being conscious and aware of eating healthily. My children understand better the benefits of gardening and eating foods that are fresh from the earth. I'll never forget watching our children, in the Louks garden, gathering the greens for that evening's salad. I loved seeing them combing the garden with baskets in hand, chewing on fresh vegetables right from the earth. We are now on the road to a vegan/raw lifestyle ourselves and are so grateful for the special time we spent in Malibu with the Louks family.

Lovingly,

Cyndi DuFur
Sun Valley, Idaho

Your testimonial is next! We look forward to hearing how our book has helped you along in your journey. Please e-mail us at: junelouks@verizon.net

Introduction: Our Family's Story: Good-bye Migraines!

An Angel

Here's my story, a good case for eating pure, living, fresh, plant food. I'm not a medical doctor or a dietician (although my only A plus while earning my BA at U.C. Berkeley was in nutrition). I am a mother of four children, with many mouths to feed. So I have made it a priority to explore and discover healthy food choices that the entire family will enjoy and ones which will positively un-impact our world.

Six o'clock in the morning, I bounce out of bed for prayer, deep breathing, meditation, and yoga. Then the girls wake up, and after some hugs and cuddles, together we whip up a green fruit smoothie with hemp seeds. Jeff packs a great lunch for them and then he and the older girls are out the door. I might meet some girlfriends for a surfing session, but most of the time I get to hang out with our four year old, Charlotte (our baby). It is great to be alive. I'm experiencing an amazing level of health and energy. People come up and ask me what I have been doing. Quarterly I will teach an "uncooking class." This last year has been full of changes, and I look at how far I have come.

Three years ago, I was in a different place. Four young children to take care of would be wonderful, except when those migraine headaches hit. (Mom, do you ever get headaches?) I had them on and off, but then they were hitting like a ton of bricks several times a month, and they lasted for days. I was waking up in pain and going to bed in pain, even if I didn't have a migraine. The pain became unbearable, and I became willing to do anything to make them go away ... even to go as far as to try raw food.

I was desperate. It looked like my alternative was heavy medication (bring on the morphine), which was a path I did not want to go down. The fine print we read on medications, with all those side effects, looked like a sure road to degeneration. However, the path I was on was also degenerating before my eyes: my vision, fatigue, and memory loss.

Enter Don Kidson. Don is an occasional visitor at our local church and has been "raw" for over twenty-five years. He is known by some as the "Juice Prophet" and by others as the "Hardware Humanitarian." He is many years young and the most radiant-looking senior at our church, full of light and warm smiles. After church, we'd chat about the week's Bible lesson, and he would start telling me that the patriarchs ate primarily raw food. Hmmm ... after a friendly disagreement, he'd go to his car and bring back a book. Another time, a book and a compact disk, or a book and a video, and so on. I'd graciously thank him, smiling, yet thinking in the back of my mind, "Why would anyone want to eat raw food?" It sounded ... unappetizing and strange.

We all have family members who have some sort of addiction, from alcohol and drugs to caffeine, sugar, and cooked food. Don shared with us that, in his opinion, all addiction is rooted in cooked (processed and denatured) food, and when we leave cooked food (including processed sugars and flours), all other addictions simply fall away.

Addictions most certainly compromise our body's ability to receive nutrients.

Our family has seen this to be true. It sounds so simple: leave cooked food and addictions fall away. But for us, this seemingly simple path took us on a purifying journey toward a more wholesome way of living and forged deeper emotional calm and spiritual strength for all of us. (See Our Family's Story, Continued, toward the back of the book.)

Pure and Simple

As Michael Pollan notes in his book, *An Omnivore's Dilemma,* as a country, we have a national eating disorder. Think about it. We drink diet sodas loaded with chemicals (called sweeteners) to avoid calories while supporting fast-food joints on multiple corners of every city and hamlet (except Ashland, Oregon) in the United States! Thirty percent of us are obese. So how can we raise our family without this compulsive disorder?

I think of this diet as a *principled practice,* or *discipline. It is not about depriving oneself—it's about the adventure of finding delicious alternatives.* When we began eating raw food, some of my friends thought I was possessed, obsessed, even starving the children. (The pediatrician checked them out recently, with flying colors. It's now proven: kids *can* survive without sugar! Plus, they have the added bonuses of more positive trips to the dentist and of not getting sick like some of the other kids at school.) Getting our children on the path wasn't easy. We have hit a lot of bumps in the road. But, hopefully, it has made these recipes even better.

When I first embarked on attempting to come up with whole, raw foods the kids would enjoy, I went to the library and checked out all the books on raw food. (I had to wait two months for some.) As I weeded through the books, I found some really good ones, and they became my springboard (and so they are listed in the references). A lot of what we learned about raw food preparation came from this study.

If the recipes look like they take a lot of time, don't be fooled. It's nothing compared to cooking (I don't have time for it). Our most delicious meals are usually the fresh produce from the backyard or the recent trip to the farmer's market. Fruit is nature's fast food, and in this day and age we all want fast food. As a parent, fruit is the easiest, most popular whole food to feed the kids. Some of our recipes take this simple approach and dress up the whole foods just a bit. (See "Sapote with Lime," "Olga's Tomatoes," "Heather's Scrumptious Purple Cabbage Delight.") Other recipes are super easy to blend. Then, after you enjoy your drink, cleanup is quick and easy. Everything just rinses. (See "Super Power Smoothies," "Hot Chocolate," all the soups, and "Chocolate Mousse Pie.") However, the more time consuming recipes lend variation and culinary delight. (See "June's Favorite Daiquiris," "Pesto Pizza," and "Chocolate—Raw!") Our staples we tend to make in bulk, which at our home, still seem to go pretty quickly. (See the cereals and "Almond Mylk," "Raw Crackers," the dressing for the "Kid's Salad," "Chocolate Chip Cookies," and "Coconut Brownie Balls.") When you are preparing these recipes, the exact amounts are not important (I seldom use measuring instruments when I prep, except—let me clear my throat—for the cayenne pepper). You can vary the recipes and expand on them easily. Plus dish cleanup is so much easier—just rinse with warm water and perhaps a little vinegar. (No more pot scrubbing. See "Raw Cleaning Product" for more cleaning ideas.) However, be warned: it does take *a whole new way of thinking*—a new culinary perspective.

You will find you have a lot more energy eating raw (blended) leaves and whole foods in general. The food is pure: full of life and light (especially the greens). Perhaps you will jump into it like my husband and I did, or perhaps you will go halfway, like our children. Either way, our world will be better off and your body will thank you. So have fun with this, and enjoy. Try the "Twenty-one-day Meal Plan" featured in the back of the book or even just one day of living foods with the Louks family.

Love and Light.

Section One: Recipes

Chapter One: Breakfast

Super Green Power Smoothie

Or Super (not quite green) Power Smoothie for the kids

Start your day with a *bang*!

2 C Frozen (or fresh) Fruit (10 Strawberries/2 Bananas is the Louks girls' favorite)
Juice of 5 Oranges (The seeds taste awful; be sure to remove them.)
    Or 2 C Filtered Water
Leaves: Collards, Kale, Nettles, Stevia, or a *variety* of whatever is on hand … a little
    or a lot, stems mostly removed
Optional "High Protein Super Foods": 1 T Hemp Seeds or Powder
                                    1 T Bee Pollen
                                    1 t Blue-Green Algae

The night before: De-seed and cut up fruit. Peel the bananas, break into chunks. Put fruit in a freezer bag, and freeze.

In the morning: Put ingredients in the blender and *blend*. If you are a raw kid, blend only if your mom has shown you how. (How long? It depends on your blender. When we finally bought a Vitamix blender, we found it would blend well in 30 seconds.) Voila! Serves 4 kids and 2 adults.

> "We have these every morning and they fill me up. Some
> mornings the smoothies are better than others. I like it
> when my sister Lauren makes it." Hailey, age 7

Mama Louks Says: Leaves are a critical part of our diet because they are *full* of nutrients, including amino acids and minerals. Even "macho men" are satisfied with these smoothies. For the kids, blend just a handful of leaves, and then pour theirs into glasses (try the blue tinted glasses if the smoothie is looking greenish) with glass straws (if you make these every morning, it saves on plastic. Glass straws are available on David Wolfe's Web site: www.sunfood.com). For the grownups, we add a few larger handfuls of leaves and blend up the parent's smoothie.

The above-mentioned super foods are rich sources of easily assimilated amino acids (proteins).

If you don't eat any green veggies now, it might take your body a few months to learn to assimilate them well. Chew the smoothie, rather than guzzle it, so that your saliva is added to the smoothie. Saliva helps to break down and lubricate food as it is digested.

Organic, frozen fruit purchased in large bags is available at some markets. Because we buy organic, we don't bother with cutting off the strawberry tops. The more greens the better. If you don't have strawberries, substitute mango, or try coconut, apple, pear, etc. My personal favorites are frozen strawberry with stevia and watercress, frozen peach with kale and grape leaves, frozen pear with bok choy, frozen blueberries with nettles, and persimmons with collards. I substitute the orange juice for water with the persimmon combos.

Banana Note: Now this may really surprise your inner Curious George—seedless bananas are a hybrid, high-glycemic food, a nutritional double whammy. Bananas are also a sweet fruit and not a great mix with citrus (especially the orange juice).

Hybrid plants are plants that would not usually be found in the natural environment. Hybrids have two different "parents" that have been forced to cross-fertilize and are usually unable to produce viable second-generation seeds. High-glycemic foods have a high concentration of sugar and often are from a hybridized-plant source. High-glycemic foods can stress the digestive system. They require more insulin for digestion than low-glycemic foods.

Chimpanzees, and, I would imagine even Curious George, prefer organic, nonhybridized bananas over conventional bananas. At the Copenhagen Zoo, it has been reported that they peel the conventional bananas, but the organic, nonhybridized banana, they eat whole—banana peel and all—and prefer them over the conventional.

So if your family can enjoy the smoothie without the hybrid banana, more power to you!

Berry Crunch Cereal
a.k.a. Everything But the Kitchen Sink Cereal

2 C	Hulled Raw Sunflower Seeds (soaked 4 hours, sprouted 24 hours)
3/4 C	Pumpkin Seeds (soaked 4 hours, refrigerated until use)
4 C	Buckwheat (soaked 15 minutes, sprouted 24 hours)
1/2 C	Berries (strawberries, raspberries, cranberries and/or blueberries; we also use dried berries, apricot and prunes, chopped finely)
1/2 C	Hemp Seeds or Sprouted Quinoa (see Tabouli recipe for simple sprouting directions)
1 1/2 C	Apple, blended
1 C	Apple, finely chopped
1 C	Dried Coconut, finely shredded
3 T	Cinnamon
1 1/2 T	Mesquite Powder
1 T	Maca Powder
1 C	Almond Mylk
1	Vanilla Bean
1 t	Stevia (dried herb)
1/2 t	Sea Salt

Day 1: Soak sunflower seeds 4 hours, then toss the water, cover with cheesecloth, and set aside. (A dark place, like a cupboard, encourages sprouting.) Soak buckwheat 15 minutes. Rinse well and set aside for 24 hours to germinate. (Your seeds can be refrigerated for up to a week).

Day 2: Soak pumpkin seeds 4 hours. Dehydrate pumpkin and sunflower seeds 3 hours at 145 degrees. Using the food processor with the "S" blade, pulse the seeds, buckwheat, dried berries until finely chopped. Stir in dried coconut and apple.

In a blender, blend apples, enough to result in 11/2 cups of blended apple. Add cinnamon, mesquite powder, maca powder, almond mylk, vanilla bean, stevia and sea salt. Pour mixture over seed mixture, stir, and let sit for 15 minutes. Spread onto Teflex sheets. Dehydrate for 2 hours at 145 degrees. Reduce temperature to 105 degrees and leave overnight.

Day 3: Serve with fresh fruit (my favorite is chopped peaches) and Hemp Mylk and a sprinkling of bee pollen, or when you are ready for the next step, a handful of fenugreek and broccoli sprouts. Really!

"This is our dad's favorite breakfast," Hailey, age 7

Mama Louks Says: Sprouting germinates the seed. The protein level increases and the nutrients multiply. *This is our all-time favorite cereal.* Most seeds, nuts, and dried fruit stay fresh for several months in the refrigerator or freezer, but it is good to move through your pantry often. When it is time to move out your storehouse, this is a great recipe to use. Our last batch of "Berry Crunch Cereal" included walnuts, sesame seeds, oats, almond flour, dried mulberries, cranberries, and raisins. Another favorite we like to add in is the prunes. We sometimes we used extra yacon syrup and created bars for the kids to take with them in their school lunches, as a great source of protein. The bars disappear quickly.

Also, oats are not for the purist because of the mycotoxins, but, if you are not yet a purist, you might enjoy substituting the buckwheat for soaked (24 hours) oat groats. 12 Grain Cereal, soaked overnight, is another great option.

Finally, sunflowers seeds start to turn bad with more than 24 hours of sprouting. If you can't get to step 2 within 24 hours, you can refrigerate the sunflower seeds to slow the sprouting process and keep them from spoiling.

Teflex Sheets: These sheets have a durable, nonstick, nonporous surface and are usually available as an option when purchasing a dehydrator (which always comes with mesh sheets). I place the Teflex sheets on top of the mesh sheets when I have gooey mixtures that would otherwise seep through the mesh.

Rah! Rah! Cereal

Berry Crunch Cereal, not yet dehydrated

We prefer the "batter" of this recipe over the finished, dehydrated version. Dehydrated foods are not as easy to digest, and the batter is a more optimum *living* food. Go ahead—top your cereal with fenugreek and broccoli sprouts, and *thrive!*

Refrigerate up to 3 days.

Mama Louks Says: If you want to ease up on the buckwheat, substitute some sprouted amaranth or millet. Both take 3 hours of soaking followed by 24 or 12 hours of sprouting, respectively.

Rah! Rah! Cereal Bars

4 C Berry Crunch Cereal, not yet dehydrated
3 T Yacon Syrup

Stir together, and follow dehydrating directions for "Berry Crunch Cereal," with 1/2 inch layers of cereal on Teflex sheets at 145 degrees for 3 hours. Then using a knife, cut shapes of the bars, remove and transfer to a mesh dehydrating sheet, and dehydrate until dry.

Mama Louks Says: These 3 cereal recipes may look like they might take a lot of time, but it's just a little time each day, for 3 days. We created these bars for the kids to take with them in their school lunches, as a great source of protein. The bars disappear quickly—they are worth the effort!

If you don't have a dehydrator, use the lowest setting on your oven ... but plan to get a dehydrator soon! Ovens "kill" your food, while dehydrators dehydrate, while keeping your food "alive."

I have found that kids tend to like sweeter foods in general. Agave nectar, yacon syrup, stevia, raw honey, and date granules (pitted and dehydrated dates, coarsely ground) sweeten the foods and can all be purchased raw. Maple syrup, maple granules, rice syrup, and malted barley are not raw, but better and healthier sweeteners than the nutrient-empty, high glycemic, refined sugar. Maple syrup is not technically raw, as the sap is boiled down to syrup (and then dried for the granules), but eating it supports the maple tree.

Sweeteners: The healthiest sweeteners are whole foods, like dates or bananas. If those don't work for the recipe, I choose raw, vegan sweeteners. My favorite is yacon syrup, with agave nectar as my second runner-up. Yacon syrup comes from the root of the Peruvian yacon plant, a distant relative of the sunflower, and has a mild, full-bodied sweetness. Yacon's a relative newcomer to the world of sweeteners, so its major drawbacks are that it's a bit pricey and can be hard to find. Agave nectar, from the Mexican agave plant, is also raw and vegan, but higher in sugar than yacon syrup. Honey can be purchased raw, but some don't consider it vegan, and maple syrup is vegan, but not raw. Finally, there is stevia, which the girls like to keep handy at the table, alongside the sea salt.

Mesquite Powder: Mesquite powder is a staple in our home. It is a high-energy food with a lightly sweet and subtly spicy flavor. We use it often, including it in "Chocolate Mylk," and as a great additive in desserts. Unfortunately, the deserts (versus desserts) are being stripped of these trees, as their wood is prized for furniture and making charcoal. Buying and eating mesquite powder supports growing more of these trees. I just purchased an 8-dollar baby tree at the Theodore Payne Foundation, a foundation dedicated to preserving native plants of California. Perhaps in a few years we will be able to dehydrate the pods and make the meal ourselves in the food processor. It will hopefully be an adventure with the girls and move us toward understanding and appreciating alternative food sources and the ecological/economic dynamic of our foods.

Almond (or Hemp!) Mylk

1/2 C	Raw Almonds soaked 12 hours (or hempseeds, Brazil nuts, or your seed or nut of choice)
2 C	Coconut Milk or Water
1 t	Cinnamon

Optional: 1 T Honey—for the kids

1 T   Mesquite Powder

1 t   Vanilla Bean (or an inch of the vanilla bean)

Blend for 2 minutes on high, strain mylk with a nut-mylk bag. Refrigerate or pour warm over cereal and berries. (Or invest in a Soybella appliance, and reduce the time it takes to make mylk to 30 seconds.) No more carting milk home from the store and adding yet more milk containers to the landfills! Enjoy!

"The mylk tastes just like regular milk." Lauren, age 10

Mama Louks Says: The mylk tastes the best when filtered through a nut-mylk bag or fine (organic!) cheesecloth if you have the time (sometimes it just doesn't happen). The Soybella is a great investment if your family eats cereal in the morning.

Unlike water, coconut milk adds natural sweetness the children like. However, considering the amount of hemp and almond mylk our family drinks, we usually forgo the coconut milk for the water and instead simply add honey as a sweetener for the kids. Our family makes a triple batch of Honey Almond Mylk and regular Hemp Mylk about twice a week. For the sake of variety, we are starting to use different nuts and seeds, depending on what we pick up at the farmer's market. Pecans work well, and the macadamia nut makes a much creamier mylk. Our current favorite is hemp mylk.

Is honey vegan? I see honey as a flower product manufactured by the bee, rather than an animal product. Let me tell you why: we are not eating the bees. Honey is nectar from the flower (bee pollen is from the flower's pollen), dried by the bee, on their tongues, and saved for food. Here on the coast of California, because it doesn't snow, the bees produce more honey than they can eat. When the hives fill, they must move and find another hive. Or bee keepers can collect this extra honey (stored for easy access on the top tray of bee friendly commercial beehives) without hurting the bees. Then the bees only have to move when the size of the bee population outgrows the hive. This saves the bees from having to move around as much. I also use honey for other reasons: our children love it, it is loaded with enzymes, and here in California, we can all buy locally harvested honey. Although the coconut water is delicious and probably healthier, it would be imported from Thailand. Raw honey is simpler to prepare and it's *local!* Buying raw honey from bee-friendly collectors supports and protects the honeybee, which needs our support right now!

"I love rah, rah, really *raw* honey!" Charlotte, age 4

Yummy French Toast

1	Loaf of Cinnamon Date Manna Bread
1 1/2 C	Almond (or Hemp!) Mylk
1/4 C	Maple Syrup
1 T	Ground Cinnamon
1/4 t	Ground Nutmeg
1/4 t	Sea Salt

Slice bread into 1/4 inch slices (this is easier when partially thawed) and set into a large glass baking dish. Blend remaining ingredients (except bread) and pour over bread. If you double the recipe, like I do, so we can have it 2 days in a row (which saves me time), add remaining bread slices for the second layer, and pour remaining batter. At any event, let sit for 1/2 hour, occasionally tilting dish and submerging bread. Place on Teflex sheets and dehydrate at 145 degrees for an hour or two. Flip bread, while removing Teflex sheet (place a mesh sheet on top of tray, and flip—you will soon become a master if your kids love this dish as much as mine do). Dehydrate at 105 degrees for 6 more hours, or longer, depending when everyone wakes up. Serve with sliced bananas, strawberries and maple syrup.

Mama Louks Says: I find Manna Bread in the frozen section of our local co-op. It was baked at a low heat, so it might not be completely raw.

We aren't big on dairy, but occasionally, Lauren, age 10, used to mix up raw cream with agave in our standing mixer and top her French Toast with this whipped cream. The smile she has while she is eating this is priceless. If your family does make whipped cream, another delightful snack is strawberries and cream. (See the "Strawberries and Cream" recipe at the end of the dessert section for a raw version of whipped cream!)

You will have leftover soak water. The kids like it plain or on their Rah! Rah! Cereal.

The more trees the better, so I like the idea of supporting the maple tree. Also, whereas refined sugar is empty calories, devoid of any nutrients, maple granules contain calcium, potassium, iron, manganese, phosphorus, B vitamins and amino acids. (According to Sun Organic Farms, "the sap of a maple tree is the liquefied nutrient the plant uses for the growth of its tissue.")

Blueberry Scones

2 C   Steel Cut Oats
3/4 C   Dates, pitted
1/2 C   Dried Blueberries (presoaked 1 hour)
1/2 C   Hemp Seeds
1/2 C   Macadamia Nut Flour (or grind macadamia nuts in the blender)

In a food processor with the "S" blade, process all ingredients, except the macadamia-nut flour, into a batter. Using the nut flour to keep your hands from getting too sticky, shape the batter into your desired scone shape. We like using a heart cookie cutter, but it can get a bit sticky, so keep the nut flour handy to dip the cookie cutter and fingers after each impression. Simple cookie shapes are easiest. The nut powder gives added texture and taste.

Set scones on a mesh dehydrator sheet. Dehydrate at 145 degrees for 2 hours, and then at 95 degrees for 8 hours. The thicker your scones, the longer dehydrating time they will need.

Mama Louks Says: This was a great transition food for us. The oats are on Dr. Cousens' list of foods with mycotoxins, so we don't make these as much now, but if you like oats, you will love this recipe. You can substitute the dried blueberries with your favorite dried fruit. We just had to share this one with you!

Ideally, this recipe would be made with sprouted oat groats. You can sprout the oat groats by soaking them for 6 hours and then letting them sit in a dark space for 2 days, rinsing them every 12 hours. Remember, whenever you sprout, the nutrients multiply.

Our farmer's market in Santa Monica has a macadamia-nut farmer who sells the nuts and the powder, fresh! Another vendor sells fresh pecans. There is something to be said for getting as much of our food as possible locally, and it tastes fresher.

Muesli and Strawberries

Not my favorite grain and not technically raw, but close, and the kids like it

Prune Butter: 1/3 C Prunes, pitted (or dried apricots) soaked a few hours

                      1/3 C Water (soak water from dried fruit enhances sweetness)

Blend!

1/2 C Boiled Water

1/2 C Muesli (uncooked; available from Sun Organic Farm) or Steel Cut Oats

Honey Almond (or Hemp!) Mylk

Sliced Strawberries

Let boiled water stand 1 minute. Mix in muesli. Cover and let stand 3 minutes. Mix in Prune Butter to taste. Add mylk and top with strawberries.

Chapter Two: Morning Snacks

Fly High Apple Pie Sandwiches
Snack time!

Apples, thinly sliced
Raw Almond Butter
Raw Cereal (see recipe)

Slice apples, spread almond butter, sprinkle with cereal, and top with second apple slice. Enjoy!

> "I like the Banana Boats and Apple Sandwiches for
> snack time at school. Yum!" Charlotte, age 4

Mama Louks Says: These are a big hit and great to serve at the kid's parties. They go quickly. Our family is not doing peanut butter anymore because of the aflatoxin present in peanut butter. Instead, as a family, we chose almond butter. I've tried a lot of different raw almond butters and my favorite is from Sunorganic.com. I'm still looking for a good almond butter that is from presoaked almonds. When the nuts and seeds are soaked, the enzyme inhibitors (toxins) are released, they get ready for germination, and they are healthier for digestion.

Banana Boats
With raspberry and blueberry smokestacks

Banana
Almond Butter
Blueberries
Raspberries

Carve out banana, like you would carve a canoe. Fill the "canoe" with Almond Butter. Decorate with berries.

Cinnamon Apples

Cut apples (any variety, Fuji work well, red are best looking)
Cinnamon

Sprinkle cinnamon on the cut apples and "whoa—la!"

"I love apples! I eat them every day," Lauren Louks, age 10

Mama Louks Says: Principal Hollis, the principal at our local public school, has watched the children eat lunch for years. He is convinced that kids are much more apt to eat fruit if it is cut up.

Power Raspberries

Raspberries
Almond Butter or Blueberries

Fill the raspberries with either almond butter or blueberries. The kids love this one!

Mama Louks Says: Raspberries can get moldy quickly. Always check the raspberries carefully for mold—and don't eat them if they are moldy.

Three years ago my grandmother helped us dig up some raspberry and blackberry shoots from her garden. We planted them on the northern side of the house, in full to partial sun, and three years later they are the jewels of the garden, generating a tremendous amount of fruit. They taste so mouthwateringly good, between the six Louks and the friends that gather to help us harvest, they have yet to even make it to the fridge. Although my grandmother is no longer with us, her legacy flourishes with her wonderful berries. A little of her Kansas farm is out the kitchen window and her farming enthusiasm continues to inspire us.

Mesquite Walnuts and Pecans

2 C   Walnuts or Pecans, soaked 1-2 hours and chopped into quarter-inch-sized chunks
2 T   Mesquite Powder
2 T   Cinnamon
1 or 2 T   Maple or Yacon Syrup (I prefer yacon syrup, if I have it on hand)
1 t   Sea Salt

In a large mixing bowl, combine ingredients, mixing in the syrup last. Spread out on a Teflex sheet and dehydrate at 145 degrees for 2 hours. Remove Teflex sheet and reduce heat to 105 degrees for 2 hours. Eat fresh or store in the refrigerator.

Mama Louks Says: When we first started snacking on nuts, the girls did not like them. This recipe helped open up the wonderful world of nuts. We still eat these as snacks, but they are also great salad toppers when guests visit for dinner.

Some people don't feel good when they feed their bodies fats and sugars together, especially diabetic and sugar-sensitive people. If you are one of these, forgo the syrup, and substitute 1/4 t of cayenne pepper.

Pumpkin Seed Crunchies

2 C   Pumpkin Seeds (soaked 4 hours)
1/4 t   Sea Salt
Optional: 2-4 T Maple Syrup

In a large mixing bowl, combine the ingredients. Spread out on a Teflex sheet and dehydrate at 145 degrees for 2 hours. Remove Teflex sheet and reduce heat to 105 degrees for 2 hours. Eat fresh or store in the refrigerator.

> The kids in my class really liked the pumpkin seeds with
> apples and pomegranates on Halloween. My mom figured
> they would get enough sugar that night." Hailey, age 7

Mama Louks Says: The children prefer the pepitas, a variation of pumpkin seeds from Central and South America, with the thinner, crunchier, green skin, but either works. And guess what—these seeds can be up to 29 percent calories from protein! Sunflower seeds can be substituted in this recipe and are another great protein source.

Chapter Three: Lunch

Raw Crackers

Our three favorites:

Buckwheat Crackers:
8 C	Sprouted Buckwheat (see cereal recipe)
1 C	Red Bell Pepper (remove seeds and stem)
1 C	Carrot Pulp (enjoy the juice while you prep)
1 C	Onions, grated
1/2 C	Broccoli (or cauliflower)
1/2 C	Spinach
1/3 C	Greens—preferably basil (or cilantro or parsley)

Sea Salt and Cayenne Pepper (1/8 t max.) to taste

Puree all ingredients in a food processor with the "S" blade till the dough is smooth. Smooth out dough to a thin layer (as thin as possible) onto the Teflex sheet that comes with your dehydrator. An easy way to do this is by covering spread with a second dehydrator sheet and rolling a rolling pin over it. Dehydrate sheets of dough at 145 degrees for 4 hours. Peel dough off Teflex sheet onto plastic mesh sheets. Next, run a table knife partly through the dough outlining your cracker sizes. As crackers start to dry, reduce dehydrator heat to 105 degrees and then continue dehydration until crackers are dry. Crackers should break off easily along the slice marks.

Spelt Crackers: 2 C Sprouted Spelt (Soak 12 hours and let sit 48 hours, rinsing daily)
1 C Carrot Pulp (left over from juicing carrots)
1 C Red Pepper
1 C Spinach
Sea Salt and Cayenne Pepper (1/8 t max.) to taste

Prepare same as above.

Topping: 1/2 C Onion, thinly sliced
4 Garlic Cloves, minced
1/3 C Basil, minced

Spread topping and dehydrate about 6 hours.

Mama Louks Says: I like to use the blank plate with the Twin Gear juicer to make the dough for these two crackers, but the Twin Gear juicer is an investment. The food processor works fine. For pizza crusts or bread, spread dough more thickly to 3/8 inch thickness. Add slices of yellow onion and several minced garlic cloves liberally to top of bread before dehydrating.

Onion Crackers: 1 1/2 C Flaxseeds (ground in a blender)
1 1/2 C Sunflower Seeds (soaked 7 hours)
3 Onions (grated or thinly sliced in a food processor)
1/3 C Extra Virgin Olive Oil
1 t Sea Salt or 1/4 C Namu Shoyu
Optional ingredients: Cayenne Pepper (just a dash)
A Handful of Parsley
Freshly Ground Black Pepper

Prepare same as above, about 1/4 inch thickness. If spreading is difficult, add a touch of warm (filtered) water. The Namu Shoyu decidedly makes this cracker taste outstanding, and I suggest it as a transition food. For optimum health, leave it out.

Mama Louks Says: We make these in large quantities each month. The Buckwheat Crackers are the best. Jeff enjoys the Onion Crackers. When you are eating raw, the Spelt Crackers give mouthwatering variety.

Spelt versus wheat: Wheat is a hybrid of spelt. Spelt is wheat without the level of gluten. So go for the "original" grain. Spelt (and buckwheat) unstored does not have mycotoxins.

In regards to the flaxseeds, which is better, gold or brown? The golden flax, although more expensive, has more nutrients, and the golden flax oil is gentle on the throat. Brown seeds add visual interest.

Easy Flax Crackers

2 1/2 C   Flaxseeds (soaked 4 hours)
4   Scallions, finely chopped
1/2   Red Bell Pepper, finely chopped
1/2 t   Herbamere

Mix, spread onto Teflex sheets and dehydrate. (Dehydrate for 2 hours at 145 degrees, remove from Teflex sheets and turn onto plastic mesh sheets, slicing crackers into squares, and then for 4 hours at 105 degrees)

Avocado with Crackers
A family staple

Buckwheat Crackers
Thinly Sliced Avocado
Sea Salt (or herbamere or hing)
Onions, grated
Purple Cabbage, grated
Sprouts (the kids like alfalfa, I like fenugreek, broccoli and sweet pea, Jeff eats
      whatever we give him)

Layer the crackers with avocado and sprinkle with sea salt or hing. Continue layering with onion and purple cabbage, and then top with sprouts.

Mama Louks Says: This recipe is simple, delicious, and quick—if you have a good month's supply of crackers premade. When we were transitioning to whole, raw foods, we would eat this almost every day with salad. This recipe, along with the fresh, local produce (well washed with filtered water), allows us to eat like royalty.

    We like to bring a good supply of these when we travel. We recently flew into Mexico, and they confiscated my organic avocados. I was panic stricken. (Standard routine, of course, when flying in and out of the continental U.S.—no produce) However, the airport official assured me I would find lots of even larger avocados in Mexico. He was right. Fortunately, he let me keep my hing and crackers.

Avo (Not So Skinny) Dip

Marinade: 1/2 White Onion, finely chopped
Garlic Cloves, minced
Slices of Fresh Ginger, minced
1/3 C Extra Virgin Olive Oil (or Hemp Oil)
3 Basil Leaves, finely chopped

Use a garlic press to mince the garlic and ginger. Combine ingredients and marinate for at least 15 minutes (can be refrigerated for up to a week). Drain the oil off, saving it for later use in salad dressings.

Avocados
1 Extra Large Scoop of Almond Butter

Mash both ingredients together with the marinade. Serve with Raw Crackers or even better, your favorite veggies: sugar snap peas, snow peas, green beans, celery, red and yellow peppers, cucumber, broccoli, cauliflower, etc. Serves 6 hungry kids, maybe.

"When our friends are over, we all have 3 dipped veggies.
Then we dip with these healthy tostado chips and then the dip
disappears really quickly." Lauren, age 10 (If Mom brings out the
chips, it's the kind with sea salt, without the trans-fats.)

"Mmm! I love that dip!" Charlotte, age 4

Mama Louks Says: Salt, table salt as we know it, has been refined, bleached, stripped of minerals, and sometimes even has sugar added. Sea salt is good, Celtic sea salt is better (more minerals), or try our favorite, the pink Himalayan salt. Himalayan salt contains the same 84 trace elements that are found in our bodies. If you are reducing your salt, Herbamere is a delicious alternative. Or, if you are moving away from salt altogether, which is best, try substituting hing.

Fresh Tomato Salsa

2 C   Tomatoes, chopped
3/4 C Fresh Cilantro, finely chopped
1/2 C Scallions, finely chopped
2 T   Fresh Lime Juice
1 T   Fresh Flaxseed Oil (or Olive Oil)
3/4 t   Ground Coriander
3/4 t   Cumin
Pinch of Cayenne Pepper

Combine ingredients and serve.

Vegan Tuna
Save the Tuna!

3 C Raw Sunflower Seeds (soaked 7 hours), ground in a food processor
5 stalks of Celery, diced
1/2 bunch of Scallions, diced
2 T Dulse Flakes
1/2 C Dried Dill

In a large mixing bowl, combine and set aside.

1 1/2 C Thai Coconut Water
3   Cloves of Garlic, pressed
1/4 C   Fresh Lemon juice
1 t   Sea Salt
2 1/2 C Macadamia Nuts or Pine Nuts

Blend thoroughly. Pour over "salad" in the large mixing bowl. Combine.

Mama Louks Says: This dish didn't start out popular, but as we modified the recipe, and introduced it a couple of times, they have grown to love it in their lunches with sprouted pita bread and sprouts or on toasted sprouted bread with avocado and romaine lettuce. If you don't have any more "tuna," the avocado/lettuce sandwich works great, too. Jeff and I enjoy Vegan Tuna with pepper scoopers (1/4 of a red, yellow, or orange pepper) with a splash of sprouts on top. Purple cabbage is also a great scooper.

Vegan Tuna Sandwich—Raw

Buckwheat Crackers
Vegan Tuna
Tomato Slices
Caesar Salad Dressing, Creamy Tahini Dressing or Avocado Dip Marinade
Tomato Slices
Dash of Hing
Sprouts (clover, broccoli or sweet pea)

Layer the sandwich in the order above, adding the dash of hing directly to the avocado. Top with sprouts. Go to heaven!

Mama Louks Says: Hing is a great alternative to garlic and onions and can be interchanged with these and all alliums throughout these recipes. Admittedly, the girls love this with avocado, although mixing avocado and other proteins like seeds is not a "proper" food combination.

Cucumber Wraps
One of June's favorites

Cucumber (thinly sliced lengthwise)
Vegan Tuna (or Nanette's Hummus)
Sliced Avocado
Purple Cabbage (thinly sliced or use fermented veggies if prepared)
Ginger (thinly sliced)
Lemon Juice and Olive Oil
Toothpicks

Combine cabbage and ginger in lemon juice and olive oil and set aside. On a cutting board or sushi press, lay two slices of cucumber side by side, overlapping by 1/4 inch. On lower half of cucumber, spread Vegan Tuna, avocado, and then cabbage/ginger combo (or fermented veggies). Roll up cucumber slices and stab with a toothpick in the middle at the overlap. Enjoy!

Mama Louks Says: Persian Cukes are our family's favorite, and an easy mono-meal!

Cucumber/Tahini Sandwich on Spelt Bread

Spelt Bread (Spelt Cracker Recipe made 3/8" thick, dehydrated 6-9 hours at most)
Sesame Tahini
Cucumber (sliced lengthwise)
Mixed Greens (and Cilantro and Basil)
Heirloom Tomato Variants
Hemp Seeds
Optional: Horseradish

Spread thin layer of tahini (or Creamy Tahini Dressing) on Spelt Bread. Layer with cucumber slices, mixed greens, and sprinkle with hemp seeds. Next layer a spoonful of Heirloom Tomato Variants. Finally top with spelt bread (spread thinly with horseradish, if you dare). Serve with salad.

Heather's Scrumptious Purple Cabbage Delight

For the onion dressing:
1/2 Onion, finely chopped
1/4 C Extra Virgin Olive Oil
Garden Herbs, Minced (oregano, basil, rosemary)
1 T Namu Shoyu or Sea Salt to taste
(a delicious protein rich alternative dressing to this is the Creamy Tahini Dressing)

Combine in a bowl and let sit for at least 15 minutes, to marinate. Drain, refrigerating liquid for a salad dressing at a later date.

Large Purple Cabbage Leaves
Sliced Avocado
Lettuce Greens
Sprouts

Fill a cabbage leaf with your favorite living foods; the list above is Heather's favorite. Sometimes she adds Nanette's Hummus, Brigitte's Unbelievable Pesto, or Vegan Tuna. Add onion dressing and then top with sprouts. Enjoy!

Strawberry Crackers

4 C   Mixed Berries
2 C   Almond Flour
1 C   Walnuts
3/4 C   Yellow Flaxseeds
1/2 C   Raisins (presoaked, 1 hour, if possible)
1/2 C   Dark Agave Nectar

Blend ingredients in a food processor. Spread onto a Teflex dehydrating sheet. Cover with a second dehydrating sheet and smooth dough out to a thin layer with a rolling pin. Dehydrate at 145 degrees for 3 hours. Remove Teflex sheet, flip onto plastic mesh sheets, and dehydrate for 8 more hours or until firm and dry.

Mama Louks Says: These crackers are great to have on hand for a quick lunch snack for the kids with almond butter and honey. At first, the girls were not too hot on them, but after 2 bites here and 2 bites there, it has become a staple. But *the* ultimate treat is having these crackers spread with hemp seed butter and topped with blueberries. Or, instead of blueberries, try sliced nectarines or apricots and a sprinkling of sprouted quinoa on top for a gourmet delight to share with your friends.

Hailey's Blackberry Burgers

Strawberry Crackers
Almond Butter (or Hempseed Butter)
Blackberries (blueberries, strawberries, apricot and peaches are also favorites)
Optional: Sprouted Quinoa (soak overnight, sprout 24 hours, dehydrate for a few
hours and eat or refrigerate)

Layer sandwich open-faced, first with a cracker, then spread the almond butter, decorate with fruit, sprinkle with quinoa, and cover with a second cracker.

> "The Blackberry Burgers are yummy! They are fun, cool, and tasty. They
> are good for the planet because we eat fewer cows. Blackberry burgers
> are healthier because burgers have white flour in the bread, sugar in the
> ketchup and salad dressing, orange cheese, the tomatoes and lettuce are
> not organic, and the French fries are really bad for you!" Hailey, age 7

Mama Louks Says: This sandwich is great if I'm packing a lunch. I omit the fruit and put it in a separate container, and then put a second cracker on top. At lunch time, just open the sandwich back up and add the fresh layer of fruit.

In the back of this book, under "Where to Find It," I share our lunch container supplier, at reusablebags.com. It's a great Web site loaded with facts to inspire anyone to think more creatively about storage containers and bags to minimize plastic bag and plastic wrap consumption.

Chapter Four:
Afternoon Delights

Jeff's Blueberry Smoothie

1 1/2 C Blueberries
3 Bananas
10 Dates (pits removed)
1C Hemp Mylk
Cacao Nibs
Goji Berries (finely chopped)
Optional: Ice

Blend, adding in ice if you'd like. Pour into glasses and top with a sprinkling of cacao nibs and goji berries.

Fruit Leathers

Seasonal Fruit

Remove seeds, and blend fruit in a blender till it liquefies. Spread mixture over a Teflex sheet, and dehydrate at 145 degrees for 3 hours. Slice into strips, remove Teflex sheet, and place leather on dehydrator rack. Reduce heat to 105 degrees and dehydrate for 3 more hours.

Mama Louks Says: More hydrating than dried fruit, fresh fruit is always better to eat, especially during the warmer months. The girls *love* fruit leathers, so I find I need to remind them to reach for the fresh fruit first, and reserve the dried fruit for when they're out of the fresh, on the road, or at school.

Orange Juice Popsicles
Squeeze it and freeze it!

1 C Fresh Squeezed Orange Juice

Pour juice into Popsicle molds, add the sticks and freeze. Simple!

Kids love these!" Heather, age 10

Mama Louks Says: This is a staple treat we like to have on hand, and a winner for other kids who come over to play. Sufas is the culinary store in town that has the Popsicle forms, and we bought a bunch. If only I could get the kids to let me add chia seeds into the popsicles, as they are also high in Omega 3 essential fatty acids (second only to flaxseeds, see *Whole Foods Companion* by Dianne Onstad, page 338). I'll keep trying! You might want to try adding some pulp back into the juice; at least the juice is not pasteurized!

Cream Popsicles

1 C Honey or Coconut Almond Mylk

Follow previous Popsicle directions.

Mama Louks Says: These are refreshing afternoon treats, and the Coconut Almond Mylk is probably better for the kids than the orange juice popsicles because, as with all juice, orange juice is more of a sugar load.

Lemonaid

Medium Pitcher of Filtered Water
Juice of 4 Lemons
4 T Agave Nectar
        Optional: 2 t Chia Seeds

Combine ingredients (let sit for 10 minutes if chia seeds are added). Add ice, and serve.

"I brought in two pitchers of 'Lemonaid' to my class for a
history project party and they liked it!" Lauren, age 10

"We have lots of sales at our lemonade stand.
They really like it with ice!" Hailey, age 7

Mama Louks Says: This is another big hit at our house. Our tradition has evolved where the parents drink lemon water, without the aid of any sweetener, fresh, with a sprinkle of chia seeds, to make one version of our Lemon Chia Seed Drink. I love this drink and find it balancing, with the protein fats in the chia seed.

The girls on the other hand, occasionally have the chia seeds, but always add the agave. Sometimes after dinner, and salads are eaten, they pass around the agave and add it to their lemon water. This combination also makes a winner of a popsicle, another staple of ours. By the way, *the kids* make the popsicles.

Lemon Chia Seed Drink

Prepare recipe for Lemonaid, adding 2 T of chia seeds, 2 inches of ginger root, juiced, and a touch of salt. Let the seeds soak for at least 15 minutes or so, till they soften.

Mama Louks Says: Chia seeds are a good source of Omega 3 essential fatty acids, as well as fiber, minerals, antioxidants and protein. These seeds have a long shelf life (5 years), so are great to keep with you on the road. Add them to your drink when you are at a restaurant, if you are hard pressed to find whole raw fats or proteins on the menu to go with your salad!

Refreshing Citrus-Rosemary Water

1 Lime (sliced)
1 Orange—zest in large strips
3 Rosemary Sprigs
3 C Filtered Water

Steep ingredients in water by refrigerating for 1 hour. Serve.

Gingeraid

2 T Grated Lemon Peel
1/2 C Ginger (juice one inch if possible and peel and chop the rest)
3/4 C Raw Honey
1/4 C Raw Agave
1/3 C Freshly Squeezed Lemon Juice
1 1/2 C Freshly Squeezed Orange Juice
6 C Filtered Water
2 C Ice
Cucumber
Mint Sprigs

Blend ingredients (except ice) for 5 seconds on high in blender, and let mixture stand for the day, ideally in the sun. Strain mixture, blend with ice, and serve in pitcher with orange and lemon slices, cucumber ribbons (cucumber cut spirally and sliced) and mint sprigs.

Mama Louks Says: This is a refreshing treat at a summer pool party. If you don't have the time to let it stand, blend and strain the ginger (in 1/2 cup of water). Add remaining ingredients, blend with ice and you are good to go. The ginger makes it a wonderfully warming drink. For an even simpler recipe, prepare like the Refreshing Citrus-Rosemary Water and steep the sliced ginger, cucumber ribbons, and mint sprigs in water, refrigerate for an hour, and serve.

"Nerds"

2 T Lemon Juice
4 T Agave Nectar (4 T = 1/4 C)
3 C Ice
Optional: 1/2 C Strawberries

Blend!

"These 'Nerds' are cool ('cool' *and* refreshing)!" Lauren, age 11

Mama Louks Says: The kids like it simple, and this is one of their favorite "staples." This recipe was created by Lauren and is easy for the kids to make.

Sapote with Lime
Better than Key Lime Pie!

1 Sapote (or Cherimoya)
1 Lime

Slice fruits. Squeeze lime juice over fruit. Enjoy! (Scoop cherimoya into your mouth with a spoon.)

Mama Louks Says: The sapote tastes best (like custard!) when it is tree ripened and eaten within a day. So the place to get sapote is from a backyard tree. Our kids enjoy most fruits best by themselves. There are a few exceptions where they like to add lime. Lime is also a winning combination with melon and papaya. The lime brings these fruits to life, and the kids then enjoy these fruits more often.

June's Favorite Daiquiris
Time to celebrate!

5 Green Apples
1 inch of Ginger
1 Lime (juiced)
Pinch of Cinnamon
1 C Ice

Serves 8

Put apples and ginger, skin and all, through a juicer (the Twin Gear juicer works great). Fill blender with mixture, lime juice, cinnamon, and ice. Blend on high for 5 seconds. Enjoy immediately or refrigerate and serve when your guests arrive. It is so delicious and warming you can skip the alcohol!

Melon Delight
Frozen melon and lime, blended to a sorbet

1 Small Melon
Juice of 1 Lime

Cut melon into cubes and freeze for 1/2 hour. Put melon into blender with lime juice. Blend and enjoy!

Mama Louks Says: A great "popsicle" alternative to this recipe that smaller children love: Cut melon into 1-inch thick strips. Give the children their favorite cookie-cutter shape and make a shape out of the melon. Stick a popsicle stick into the shape, put it in the freezer for an hour, and you have another Melon Delight.

Watermelon Pizza

1 Watermelon

Using your largest knife, cut one of the "noses" off the watermelon. Continue slicing 1/2 inch thick "pizza rounds" (or 1 inch for deep-dish pizza) as you need them. Laying a round flat on a cutting board, carve out the watermelon slice, removing the rind. Then slice round into 6 pizza shaped slices, following the natural lines of the watermelon.

Serves up to 2 soccer teams, depending on the size of the watermelon.

Easy Banana Ice Cream

2 Bananas, sliced in 2 inch chunks and frozen
1 T Almond Mylk (or water)
Optional: 1 t Cinnamon
               1 t Vanilla Extract or 1/2 Vanilla Bean
               1 T Raw Almond Butter
               2 t Raw Cacao Powder

Blend until creamy. (Serves 2)

Easy Sorbet

1/2 C Freshly Squeezed Orange Juice
2 C Fresh Fruit (with a mango and fresh berries if possible)

Blend, freeze for 2-3 hours, and serve.

Persimmon Sorbet

2 C Frozen Persimmon (de-seeded)
1/2 C Freshly Squeezed Orange Juice

Blend until creamy. Serve with a mint leaf. (Serves 4)

Pear Sorbet

2 C Frozen Pear
1/2 C Pear
Strawberry

Place pear and then frozen pear in blender. Blend until creamy. Serve in a bowl topped with a strawberry. (Serves 4)

Chapter Five: Dinner

Kids' Salad
By Lauren Louks—kids love it!

1 Head of Romaine Lettuce broken into little bits
1 Cucumber, chop only if your mom says it's O.K.
3 T Hemp Seeds
Caesar Salad Dressing to taste

Toss and enjoy!

Caesar Salad Dressing:
    1/2 C Extra Virgin Olive Oil (or Walnuts, soaked 1 hour)
    1/2 C Hemp, Sesame Seed or Freshly Pressed Flaxseed Oil
    1/2 C Filtered Water
    2 T Pumpkin Seeds
    1/4 C Spinach
    2 Garlic Cloves
    2 Celery Sticks
    1/4 C Freshly Squeezed Lemon Juice
    2 t White Miso (un-pasteurized)
    4 Dates (remove seeds)
    2 t Dulse or Kelp Granules
    1/8 t Freshly Ground Pepper
    1/2 t Sea Salt

Put ingredients in your blender and blend. Apply (all salad dressings) sparingly to salad for a kid-tested winner!

> "One time, my mom brought salad to my (pre)school. It was letter 'L' day. She brought **L**ettuce (Kid's Salad). Almost everyone ate it, and then they wanted more, and more! Some of the kids cried because there wasn't any more." Charlotte, age 4

Mama Louks Says: We have made a double batch of this every week since we began eating raw. The kids love it and the hemp seeds are a great protein source(33 percent!). If you seal it tightly and refrigerate, the dressing should last you the whole week. If it looks like we won't last the week, we add chopped scallions, apple cider vinegar or lemon juice, and sometimes more fresh flax oil to stretch it. Sometimes it's even better this way.

Our pediatrician encourages us to eat a salad the *size of our head each day!* If we put stronger leaves in our breakfast smoothie and eat our salad and crunchy veggies each day (celery, cucumbers, and peppers) this is possible. For our children!

Easy Dressing

1/4 C Filtered Water
1 T Apple Vinegar
2 T Ginger, grated
2 Garlic Cloves
1/2 C Basil
1 T Agave
Pinch of Sea Salt

Blend!

Mama Louks Says: Try this on zucchini pasta (zucchini that has been put through a Saladacco or mandoline)—delicious!

Creamy Tahini Dressing

1/3 C Caesar Salad Dressing (See Kid's Salad)
1 T Raw Sesame Tahini

In a small bowl, mash ingredients together with a fork or mortar and pestle.

Mama Louks Says: This is one of my favorite dressings on sandwiches, and it is rich in amino and fatty acids.

The McMillan Dressing

2 T Organic Extra Virgin Olive Oil

1 T Pro-Omega Liquid Oil (Nordic Naturals), Organic Hemp Seed Oil (Nutvia), or Udos Oil

2 T Apple Cider Vinegar

Honey to taste (Ron's favorite honey is White Gold raw Canadian honey)

    Optional: Bio-K Acidoophilus (a probiotic with the consistency of yogurt)

Whisk together and mix into your favorite salad.

Mama Louks Says: This dressing offers a great omega alternative to flaxseed oil and can include enzyme rich probiotics. It's a staple for the Connie McMillan/Ron Von Hagen family. I asked Connie what she does for protein, and she said one of her favorite sources is chlorella tablets. She will chew on 12-15 of them daily, like chewing on grass or alfalfa, but loaded with the protein. One of Ron's favorite sources of protein is a blended mixture of germinated/sprouted sunflower seeds, pumpkin seeds, sesame seeds, and almonds. This is a great addition to the salad.

For anyone looking for an alternative to fish oils, you may want to try Udo's DHA Oil Blend. It has the long chain fatty acids from algae (the same source the as the fish's).

Super Simple Salad

Salad Greens and everything but the kitchen sink (chopped tomato, cucumber, finely
     chopped cauliflower)
1 Avocado, chopped
Sprouts (Lentils, broccoli, fenugreek)
Pine Nuts, Hemp Seeds, or Sprouted Quinoa (soaked 3 hours and sprouted 24 hours,
     dehydrated 2 if possible at 95 degrees) or chopped walnuts, pecans, or
     sunflower seeds.
Seaweed (presoaked for 3 hours, or at least 15 minutes)
Cracker Crumbs (see cracker recipes; buckwheat crackers are my favorite crumbs;
     there are usually lots of crumbs at the bottom of our cracker bags.)

Dressing: Drizzle Extra Virgin Olive Oil
              Squeeze Lemon

Combine your selection of salad options. Add dressing. Toss and enjoy!

Mama Louks Says: For extra power-packed nutrients, try sprouting broccoli. Soak broccoli
seeds overnight. Germinate for up to four days in a sprout bag, rinsing morning and night.
Lentil sprouts are 26 percent protein.

Kelp Noodle Salad

1 C Kelp Noodles
1 Red Pepper, finely chopped
1 Tomato, finely chopped
1/4 C Cilantro, finely chopped
1/4 C Basil, finely chopped
2 T Pine Nuts
3 T Ginger, finely chopped
3 T Onion, finely chopped
3 T Scallions, finely chopped
2 T Flaxseed Oil
2 Garlic Cloves, minced
1 t Oregano

Mix ingredients and serve!

Mama Louks Says: Enjoy this dish with a salad or on a cracker. The Kelp Noodles from Sea Tangle are made by removing the skin of the kelp and processing the inside at under 100 degree heat. Sodium alginate is added, which is a salt extracted from a brown seaweed.

Chinese Chic Salad

2 large handfuls of Leaves (Spinach or Arugula are my favorites with a splash of
    chickweed, but the kids like it best with Romaine Lettuce)
1/2 Jicama, sliced
4 Green Onions, chopped
1/2 C Sesame Seeds (ideally soaked 4 hours)
5 Tangerines (peeled and separated)
1/2 C Almonds (blanched and slivered)

Salad Dressing:
    1/4 C Sesame Seed Oil
    2 T Apple Cider Vinegar
    1 inch Ginger, peeled and minced
    1 Clove of Garlic
    1/4 t Sea Salt
    1/4 t Freshly Ground Pepper
    Agave Nectar to taste

Break up leaves into bite sizes and combine with salad ingredients. In a separate glass jar, combine salad dressing ingredients, secure lid, and shake vigorously. Add dressing just prior to serving.

Mama Louks Says: This is an option to the Kids' Salad, but unfortunately my kids don't like much variation to their salad. Usually, for the adult's salad, Jeff and I chop up whatever is in season and add the Caesar Salad Dressing so that we can have a fresh change.

Arugula Salad

1 Bunch of Arugula
1 Pear (or apple), chopped into small chunks
1 Avocado, chopped
1/4 C Mesquite Walnuts or Pecans

Toss ingredients with dressing. Enjoy!

Dressing:
1/4 C Finely Sliced Purple Onion
2 T Extra Virgin Olive Oil or Freshly Pressed Flax Oil
1 T Agave Nectar
1 t Mesquite
1 t Hing
1/4 t Sea Salt

Mix last five ingredients vigorously. Add the purple onion. Marinate for at least 15 minutes.

Strawberry Spinach Salad

1 Bunch of Spinach
1/2 Basket of Strawberries
1/4 C Mesquite Pecans (or Raw Pecans)
1 T Poppy Seeds
1 T Broccoli Sprouts (soak seeds overnight, sprout up to 2 days, rinsing daily)

Toss with small amount of dressing. Enjoy!

Dressing:
1/2 C Extra Virgin Olive Oil
1/4 C Raspberry Vinegar
1/4 C Agave Nectar
1 T Raw, Dried Stevia
1/2 t Dry Mustard

Mix vigorously. Refrigerate remaining dressing.

Tabouli

3 C Sprouted Quinoa (soaked 1 C for 3 hours and sprout for 24 hours)
2 Heirloom Tomatoes, chopped
3 Cucumbers, chopped (Persian cucumbers are our favorites)
2 Green Onions (thinly sliced)
6 Leaves of Mint, chopped
1/2 C Basil, finely sliced
1/2 Bunch of Parsley, stems removed and sliced

Dressing:

2 T Extra Virgin Olive Oil
1/4 t Sea Salt
1/2 t Freshly Ground Pepper
Juice of 1/4 Lemon

Serves 10

Mix dressing together. Put remaining ingredients in a large bowl. Mix in dressing.

Mama Louks Says: This is an easy, satisfying dish to make. To save time, instead of chopping individually, try chopping the 3 cucumbers at the same time with a large chef's knife. The more you can put under the knife at the same time, the more time you can spend cuddling up with your kids and a good book. Serve on the side with the Pesto Pizza at your next get-together.

Olga's Heirloom Tomatoes

3 Heirloom Tomatoes, thickly sliced
2 T Extra Virgin Olive Oil or Freshly Pressed Flaxseed Oil
2 T Basil, minced
1 Garlic Clove, minced
4 T Onion, minced
1/2 t Ginger, minced
1/4 t Sea Salt

> Optional: 1/2 t Balsamic Vinegar (not technically raw) or Apple Cider Vinegar
> (technically raw)
> 1 zucchini, thinly sliced
> 2 T Sunflower Seeds
> 4 T Sunflower Sprouts

Lay tomatoes on a large plate. If you'd like to add zucchini slices, place them over the tomato slices. Combine remaining ingredients (except sunflower seeds and sprouts) in a small bowl and pour over tomatoes. Garnish with sunflower seeds and sunflower sprouts—isn't it easy and delicious being raw?

Mama Louks Says: For easy, finely cut ginger, grate ginger when it is frozen. Ginger will store in an airtight container for approximately 2 months.

Guacamole

2 Avocados, mashed
1 Tomato, finely chopped in small cubes
1 Small Onion, finely chopped
1 T Lime Juice
1 T Cilantro, finely chopped
1/2 t Sea Salt

Squeeze lime over avocado. Combine remaining ingredients. (Serves 4)

Mama Louks Says: Spread over buckwheat crackers for delicious ice-breaking hors d'oeuvres for "raw skeptical" hungry guests. With a salad, this is a staple, anytime meal.

Spring Rolls
Lettuce wraps!

Romaine Lettuce Leaves
Cucumber, thinly sliced lengthwise
Red Pepper, thinly sliced lengthwise
1 C Cauliflower
1/2 C Broccoli
1/4 C Kale
Guacamole

Blend cauliflower, broccoli and kale until finely ground. Take one fresh lettuce leaf. Fill with a few cucumber and pepper slices. Dollop Cauliflower mixture and Guacamole and spread along the center line of the leaf. Roll up and enjoy! (Serves 4)

Summer Sushi

With a raw nori Sheet spread out, at one end, layer the same ingredients as with the Spring Rolls (except instead of guacamole, substitute the Caesar Salad Dressing). Spread Sushi Dressing (see below) on top. Then, roll up entire "enchilada." (I use a bamboo press I purchased at Sufas to help me get a tight roll.) Wet the far end of the seaweed so that it sticks and set the sushi on the damp side. Slice and serve.

Sushi Dressing:
1/2 t Apple Cider Vinegar
1 t Namu Shoya
2 T Tahini
2 T Miso
2 T Flax Oil
1 Tomato
2 T Filtered Water

Blend ingredients above in the blender and then mix in:
1 Green Onion, finely chopped
1/2 t Ginger, finely chopped
5 Basil Leaves, finely chopped

Combine and set aside for at least 8 minutes.

Variations:

Winter Sushi: roll Summer Sushi in cooked* brown rice like a snowball

Spring Sushi: add nasturtium flowers

Fall Sushi: roll the Winter Sushi in sesame seeds so that they are brown and seedy. (You can sprout sesame seeds by soaking them for 4 hours and letting them sit a day or two.)

Mama Louks Says: Namu Shoyu is a raw alternative to soy sauce, but still containing mycotoxins. In most of these recipes I substitute sea salt for Namu Shoyu, but in the case of sushi, it is hard to forgo a much loved favorite. Keep in mind, you might want to go easy on the soy sauce. Also, for a culinary twist, add some freshly minced ginger into the salad dressing. Yum!

It's always important to wash your fruits and vegetables well if they have come from the market. When making the sushi, be sure your leaves have been dried well. Only the leaves should touch the seaweed. This keeps this recipe from becoming mushy.

Another real simple favorite is wrapping collard greens or kale in avocado, dipping it in the Caesar Dressing, and adding a touch more sea salt. You just have to try it—it's delicious!

*Cooked brown rice is a good transitional food on the path towards raw. Cooked grains in general are a staple in our American diet, but they are acidifying and pull calcium from our bodies to digest.

Seaweed is a rich source of natural iodine. Since we no longer feed the kids salt with iodine added, I encourage seaweed snacks.

Sweet Potato Fries

2 Sweet Potatoes
1/2 t Sea Salt
Extra Virgin Olive Oil

In a food processor or mandolin, slice sweet potato. Then chop into French fries. Put fries in a bowl, add very warm water, mix in sea salt, and soak for 5 minutes. Then, discard water and mix in a light drizzle of olive oil. Put on mesh dehydrator sheets and dehydrate for 2 hours or more at 95 degrees. Serve with juice-sweetened ketchup.

Mama Louks Says: You can make your own ketchup, but I found it only stayed fresh for a few days. Our local co-op and Whole Foods have agave sweetened ketchup (Organicville) that keeps much longer, and the kids like it better.

This is a great way to prepare warmed vegetables. We use this same approach with corn on the cob, broccoli, and asparagus. We served the corn on the cob at Thanksgiving dinner.

Nanette's Hummus

1 C Cashews
1 Handful of Parsley
2 Garlic Cloves
1/4 C Extra Virgin Olive Oil
1 t Namu Shoyu (or Sea Salt)
Sea Salt and Pepper to taste
Optional: 1 Red Pepper, finely chopped

Mix in a food processor until smooth. Our kids like this with sprouted pita bread and sprouts. It's also great served with crudités (broccoli, celery, red peppers, sugar snap peas, and purple cabbage) or Raw Crackers.

Mama Louks Says: Let me tell you about Nanette. Nanette is a dear friend and surfing buddy and you'll see Nanette's name peppered throughout this book. When I first embarked on this raw adventure, I didn't know what to eat, but intuitively felt a healing response to eating leaves. I hadn't yet learned the brilliant concept of blending, and the leaves were taking a good amount of time to chew. So during my first few "raw days," I kept a handful of leaves in the car with me to chew while I pondered how in the world anyone could survive on raw food. My first raw day, I pulled up to meet the "Surf Mamas" (our small, dedicated group of surfing moms), and I had a stash of radish tops near the console of my car. Nanette leaned in to offer a friendly hello, and asked me what the leaves were for. I told her that I was reading about raw food and was playing with the idea of changing my diet. Nothing else was said, as I wasn't inclined to talk much about something I really didn't understand. We continued with our weekly surf sessions. Three months later, I discovered that she's out on her own raw path, inspired by our brief discussion! So, for the record, Nanette is an awesome, mostly raw surf mama, who has 2 small children. Nanette has created amazing masterpieces of her own, some of which are included in this book.

Olga's Hummus

1/4 C Pumpkin Seeds (presoaked 4 hours)
1/2 C Sunflower Seeds (presoaked 4 hours)
1 Peeled Carrot
1 Kale Leaf
1/4 C Fresh Basil
1 t Dried Cilantro
1/2 t Dill
1/2 t Trocomere (a relative of Herbamere)
1/4 t Freshly Grated Pepper

Blend ingredients in a food processor with the "S" Blade. Enjoy!

Mama Louks Says: This is delicious as a spread in sandwiches, sushi, and cucumber wraps!

Gazpacho Verde

5 Tomatoes
1 C Celery Juice
3 T Lemon Juice
2 Scallion Stalks
1 Jalapeño, seeded
2 Cucumbers
1 Zucchini, small
2 T Cilantro
2 Garlic Cloves
Herbamere to taste

Combine ingredients in a food processor with an "S" blade for 10 seconds (do not puree). Refrigerate at least 2 hours.

Mama Louks Says: Keep a double recipe of this chilled by the pool on a warm summer day, and enjoy all afternoon!

Sweet Pea Soup

20 Pea Shoots (Pea Sprouts)
1 C Filtered Water
2 t Olive Oil (or 1 T Avocado)
1/2 C Spinach
2 T Chopped Leeks
1/2 Small Zucchini

Blend until warm. (Serves 2)

Zucchini Soup

1 1/2 C Zucchini (chopped)
1 C Filtered Water
2 t Extra Virgin Olive Oil (or Hemp Oil), or 1 T Avocado
2 Garlic Cloves
4 Basil Leaves
1/4 t Chile Pepper
1/4 t Sea Salt

Blend until warm. Enjoy! (Serves 4)

Living Tomato Soup

6 Large Tomatoes
6 Pieces of Sun Dried Tomatoes (presoaked for 1/2 hour in 1 C water)
1/2 Avocado
1 C Water
1/2 T Olive Oil
1/4 C Basil
1/4 C Cilantro
2 Garlic Cloves
2 Large Celery Stick, chopped into chunks
1t Raw Honey
1/2 t Sea Salt or Herbamere

Sea Salt to taste

Place all the ingredients in the blender, including the sundried tomato soak water, and blend for 11/2 minutes or until nice and warm. Add bean sprouts (for "noodles"), sunflower sprouts, sliced avocado, diced bell pepper or cilantro for garnish.

Mama Louks Says: This is a kid favorite and simple to make. Lauren, age 10, usually makes it for us with her salad and sprouted grain toast.

Heirloom tomatoes make ugly beautiful. They aren't picture perfect like tomatoes we find in most grocery stores. They have richer, deeper colors. However, once you try an heirloom tomato, it is difficult to go back. The richness and the depth of an heirloom is incomparable.

Another great tomato dish is to create a mixture of olive oil, chopped basil, pine nuts, and salt and pour over your sliced heirloom. It is mouthwatering deliciousness.

Green Soup

1 Extra-Large Handful of Greens (spinach is delicious)
3 Stalks of Celery, chopped in chunks
1 Cucumber, chopped in chunks
1 Bell Pepper
1 Avocado
1/4 C Filtered Water
1 Garlic Clove
1 Tomato
Juice of 1/4 Small Lemon

Blend and serve cool, or blend for 2 minutes and serve nice and warm.

Mama Louks Says: These two soups are more enjoyed by big people. The Green Soup is a great option if you miss your morning Super Green Power Smoothie.

If your guests have a history of kidney stones, you might want to avoid spinach, Swiss chard, beet tops, New Zealand spinach, poke, purslane, and lamb's quarters, due to the high level of oxalic acid.

Super Simple Soup
Wilted or blanched veggies

If you'd like to steam your veggies, you might like to try this:

4 C Filtered Water
2 Heads of Broccoli (or Cauliflower)
1 Bunch of (skinny) Asparagus
1/2 C Spinach (or other green, leafy veggie)
3 Stocks of celery (thinly sliced)
3 Scallions, thinly sliced
2 T Organic Vegetable Broth Powder
2 t Hing (as an option to onions and garlic)
1 T Dark Un-pasteurized Miso
Optional: Sprouted Quinoa (soak 3 hours and then sprout 24 hours)
           Spelt Macaronis or Mini Soba Noodles (not raw for the kids)
           1 T Ginger (minced)
           Thinly Sliced Coconut Flesh

Prepare all your ingredients and have ready on a cutting board, with your veggies chopped into pieces no larger than a half of an inch. Turn on the vent and light up the neglected stove! Bring a pot of filtered water to boil (using a stainless steel pot). Turn off the heat and let water stand for a minute. Add the ingredients (except the noodles if you want; we save these just for the kids). Cover for 3 minutes, and whaa-la! (It's better than microwaving. Toss out that microwave if your family will let you.) If the kids want to have whole-grain noodles, cook them separately, and pour the soup over your children's noodles.

Mama Louks Says: Rather than "steaming" your vegetables, get the steam going, but then turn the heat off just before you add your vegetables. Let the veggies sit in the steam for 3 minutes or so and you are done! No water boiling over and no overcooked veggies (I used to be pretty dangerous in the kitchen).

To blanch veggies, after wilting them, put them in cold water to help seal off the cooking process and lock in the nutrients. This works well if you are serving the dish later.

I will join the family in enjoying this warm dish, without the cooked noodles.

Thai Soup

Blended ingredients:
1 C Thai Coconut Water
2 C Filtered Water
1/4 C Macadamia Nuts (soaked 2-4 hours)
1/4 C Pine Nuts (soaked 2-4 hours)
3 Cloves of Garlic
1 t Curry Powder (or 2!)
1/2 t Cumin
Pinch of Sea Salt
Optional: Stalk of Lemon Grass (chopped, preblended with the filtered water, and strained)
Thai Lime Leaf

Garnish:
1/2 C Hijiki Seaweed (soaked 2-4 hours)
1 T Lime (just the skin, grated)
2 T Basil, finely chopped
2 T Cilantro, finely chopped
1 T Namu Shoyu
1 Chili Pepper (or Red Pepper), finely chopped

Blend blended ingredients until nice and warm. Garnish with diced bell pepper, minced mint, and cilantro leaves, thinly sliced avocado, scallions and/or purple onion. For a finer texture, premake nut mylk (blend the 2 C water and macadamia nuts and pine nuts) and strain through a nut mylk bag or Soybella.

Mama Louks Says: The Thai soup is one of my favorites—having Thai soup is like "having cake and eating it too," "being raw and eating Thai food." If you can find a Thai lime leaf, blend it into the soup for extra *pizzazz!*

Thai Pizza
Great for a "make-your-own-pizza" party!

Round Spelt Bread topped with Onion and Garlic (see recipe)
Raw Heirloom Tomato Tapenade (see recipe)
Nanette's Hummus
Salad Greens
Sprouts

For the salad dressing:
1/2 Avocado
Scallions (2 shafts)
1/4 C Basil, finely chopped
1/2 Inch of Ginger, peeled
1/2 Inch of Lemon Grass
1 Thai Lime Leaf
Optional: 1 T Namu Shoyu (or Sea Salt to taste)

Blend and strain with a fine strainer.

Spread a *thin* layer of tapenade on your round cracker. Add either Nanette's Hummus or Avocado slices (Brigitte's Pesto also works great). Top with salad greens, dressing, and sprouts.

"This is my all-time favorite pizza!" Lauren, age 11

Mama Louks Says: Raw Pizza is great fun for the whole family. The children like it with Raw Goat Cheese (grated) and a traditional tomato sauce. Also, the blanched kale and zucchini on traditional tomato sauce and a sprinkling of goat cheese has made a hit. Prepare the spelt dough in pizza rounds (6-inch diameter is plenty per person, as this dish is quite filling). If you don't have any spelt bread or crackers on hand, you can substitute the crust with a cabbage or kale leaves.

You can also purchase tomato tapenade. We have the Happy Girl Kitchen Company's tapenade stocked in the raw section of our local co-op.

Primo Pesto Pasta

For the Brigitte's Unbelievable Pesto:
1 C Pine Nuts
1/3 C Shelled Hempseed
2 Cloves Garlic
1/8 C Extra Virgin Olive Oil
1/4 C Fresh Basil
Handful of Italian Parsley
1/4 t Herbamare
Optional: 2 T Nutritional Yeast
             1/4 t Sea Salt to taste

Using an "S" blade in the food processor, blend the nuts, hempseed, garlic, and olive oil. (Do not over-process these ingredients as they can become too pasty.) Add and puree the basil and parsley. Finally, add the Herbamere, nutritional yeast, and sea salt.

> "Pesto is very flexible and can be varied according to taste.
> Our family loves 4 cloves of garlic, salty and cheesy pesto.
> Others may choose to use 1 clove of garlic or no nutritional
> yeast at all, so enjoy your creativity!" Brigitte Robindore

For the Pasta:
Zucchini
Extra Virgin Olive Oil
Sea Salt

Slice into paper-thin linguini strips using a knife or mandolin (or, if you have a Saladacco slicer, even better.) You will be able to create amazing "angel-hair pasta" that will fool even a diehard pasta lover. In a bowl, gently mix in a drizzle of oil and a few pinches of salt. Dehydrate for 2 hours at 120 degrees.

Mama Louks Says: My kids prefer the "pasta" without the pesto sauce. Jeff and I and our friends like the pesto as the dressing for our evening salad, topped with the pasta. Broccoli dipped in pesto makes a great appetizer.

Garlic Lover's Cream Cheeze

2 C Sprouted Sunflower Seeds (soak 4 hours, sprout for 24 hours or less, use immediately)
3/4 C Water
2 Large Garlic Cloves
1 t Sea Salt
1 T Chopped Chives

Blend sunflower seeds, water, garlic, and salt. Pour into serving dish and sprinkle with chives.

Cheeze

Ingredients: Garlic Lover's Cream Cheeze, hold the chives. Substitute hing for garlic.

Take a large cheese cloth and wrap one layer over the top of a medium-sized bowl, tying a knot under the bowl to hold the cheese cloth tight. Pour Cream Cheeze onto cheese cloth; the cheese-making process has begun! Cover and let stand at room temperature for up to 4 hours or until ready to serve and cover. Liquid from the cheese will continue to drain into the bowl. If you are preparing Cheeze for the next day, put contraption into the refrigerator. The cheese will continue to drain for up to 18 hours. When ready to serve, place on a serving plate and sprinkle with chives.

Artichoke Hearts and Vegetable "Variantes"

3 Artichoke Hearts and peeled stems, chopped
3 Celery Stalks (chop into 1-inch sizes)
2 Carrots, sliced
1 Red Pepper, chopped
1/2 Cauliflower, chopped
1 Lemon, sliced
Juice of 1/2 lemon
2 t Sea Salt
Extra Virgin Olive Oil or Fresh Flaxseed Oil

Fill jar with ingredients, adding olive oil last, filling the jar with it. Seal tightly and refrigerate. Shake Variantes daily for one week. (Don't open for a week.) Strain and refrigerate oil for later use in a salad dressing. Serve on a bed of mixed greens. Refrigerate after opening.

Mama Louks Says: Our family loves artichokes, and I wonder what nutrients are left after 45 minutes of normal steaming. Here is an option for being able to enjoy the flavorful hearts with the life still in them. This recipe came from my Moroccan girlfriend, Lydia Amar. Lydia remembers watching her mother make this recipe when she was young. She and her 6 brothers and sisters would gather round and they would snap the petals off the artichoke hearts and eat the tips raw. With each petal, as they got closer to the heart, the tips would be more and more flavorful. It was a good pastime as they watched the sunset: "Instead of eating Cheetos, we'd sit around and snap artichoke leaves off and eat them before they turned black. Then my mom would chop up the hearts for the Variantes."

Heirloom Tomato Variantes

1 1/2 C Dried Heirloom Tomatoes
1/3 C Extra Virgin Olive Oil
2 Onion (finely sliced or chopped)
1 t Dried Basil
1/4 t Sea Salt
1/4 C Fresh Basil
1/4 C Fresh Oregano
Optional: Additional herbs (including parsley) on hand.

Thinly slice the dried tomatoes. (You can put them in the food processor with the slicing blade, and hand slice the remaining strays.) Press tomatoes into a small jar, layering tomatoes with onions, dried basil, fresh herbs, and sea salt. Add olive oil to the brim of the jar. Seal the cap tightly and shake well. Set aside for about a week. Give the jar a shake every day or so. The tomatoes will begin to soften even after a few hours, and you can use them, but it is best to wait a week or two. Strain oil and serve. Refrigerate after opening.

Heirloom Tomato Tapenade

Jar of Heirloom Tomato Variantes
1/4 C Fresh Basil

Drain oil from jar and set aside. Put the Heirloom Tomato Variantes in the food processor with the fresh basil. You may want to keep a few leaves for a garnish or for the Pesto Pizza. Don't toss the oil—it is delicious! Use the oil in your next salad with a squeeze of lime.

Pesto Pizza

Raw Crackers, cut in 4-inch circles
1 C Brigitte's Unbelievable Pesto
1/2 C Cheeze
3 T Heirloom Tomato Variantes
2 T Basil, thinly sliced
2 T Olives, thinly sliced (Moroccan Olives are my favorite)

Serves 6-10 people

Both the buckwheat and spelt crackers are delicious in this recipe. I prefer the light flakey texture of the Buckwheat Crackers. When making the Buckwheat Crackers for pizzas, I roll the dough a little thicker, so that the cracker doesn't crumble under the weight of the pizza ingredients. The Spelt Cracker works beautifully in this recipe because it holds its shape and doesn't break easily. When making your crackers, after 2-3 hours of dehydrating, use the mouth of a 3 to 4 inch jar as a "cookie cutter" to outline the crackers. When your crackers are finished dehydrating, the cracker should snap off along the line of the circle easily. Set aside the remaining cracker crumbs as "croutons" for a salad.

With a knife, spread Brigitte's Unbelievable Pesto over the pizza cracker. Then, spread some Cheeze over the Pesto. Sprinkle a few tomatoes from the Heirloom Tomato Variantes, along with some olive and basil bits and serve!

Mama Louks Says: This pizza is amazing and a great dish to serve at a party.

Lasagna

Cheeze:
  1 C Pine Nuts (soaked 4 hours or more)
  2 T Lemon Juice
  2 T Nutritional Yeast
  1 Garlic Clove (small)

Mix in a food processor until creamy and set aside.

Tomato Sauce:
  1 C Dried Tomatoes (Soaked 1 hour)
  1 Large Tomato
  1 T Lemon Juice
  2 t Olive Oil

Blend and set aside.

Vegetables:
  1 Large Zucchini (thinly sliced, with a mandolin if possible)
  1 Head of Broccoli, chopped
  1 C Spinach or Chard
  1 C Basil

Lightly steam zucchini, broccoli, and greens for 1 minute (to soften). Layer zucchini, then cheese, basil, tomato sauce, broccoli, and greens. Layer again with same ingredients and then top with a final layer of zucchini. Dehydrate at 145 for at least 1/2 hour. Enjoy!

Zucchini Wraps

  1 Large Zucchini, thinly sliced, lightly steamed
  1/2 C Basil
  1/2 C Walnuts
  1 Tomato
  1/4 C Scallions, finely chopped
  1 Fresh Garlic
  1/2 t Chili Powder
  1/2 t Cumin

Combine ingredients in a food processor, except zucchini, and then spread mixture on the zucchini slices and roll it up.

Chapter Six: Dessert

Chocolate Mylk

1 C Almond Mylk (refrigerated)
1 C Coconut Water (water from 1 refrigerated coconut)
2 1/2 t Cacao Powder
2 t Cinnamon
2 Dates (pitted)
1 t Vanilla

Blend briefly and enjoy cold.

Hot Chocolate

2 C Almond Mylk
10 Cacao Beans or 2 T of Cacao Powder
1/4 Vanilla Bean
4 Dates (pitted)

Optional: 1 T Maca Powder
1 T Mesquite Powder
1 T Hemp Oil (or Flaxseed Oil)
1 T Carob Powder (reduce cacao by half if adding carob)
1 T Tocotrienols (Raw Rice Bran Solubles, sunfood.com)

Put ingredients in blender and blend. If you are using a Vita-Mix, it will be hot in 11/2 minutes.

Mama Louks Says: I love to load up all the optional ingredients, nix the agave, and munch on the cacao beans while I make it. Try one! This is a great midnight snack. I have this several times a week, especially after dinner. With cacao, versus chocolate, the caffeine is minimal, so you can sleep like a well-fed baby.

Date Shake

2 C Almond Mylk
1 1/2 Frozen Bananas
3 Dates

Blend and enjoy!

"I like it cold. It's delicious!" Lauren, age 10.

Vanilla Ice Cream
By Hailey Louks

6 Dates (pitted)
1/2 T Raw Honey
2 C Honey Almond Mylk
1/4 C Macadamia Nuts
1 t Hempseeds
Vanilla Bean

Blend until creamy. Pour into ice cream maker. Enjoy when ready. (An alternative to using an ice cream maker is to freeze the blended liquid first. Then cut frozen cream into chunks and "cream" chunks in the blender or through the Twin Gear juicer with the blank plate.)

Serves 4

Mama Louks Says: This is a "Hailey Original." I wanted to add more hempseeds and pistachios, but Hailey held firm. So here it is!

Strawberry Ice Cream
Another "Hailey Original"

Same as previous recipe, only add 2 baskets of organic, washed strawberries. Serves 6.

Jeff's Dream Mint Ice Cream

1 1/2 C Coconut Meat
1/4 C Pistachios
7 Dates, pitted
1/4 C Coconut Water
1/4 Vanilla Bean
1/4 C Mint Leaves
1/2 t Mint Extract

Blend until creamy, chill, or pour into ice-cream maker.

Mama Louks Says: If your ice-cream maker needs to be pre-chilled, make sure you put it in the freezer the day before. If it is a small container, only put half the liquid in at a time. If you don't have an ice-cream maker, you can freeze it first and then put it through your juicer with the blank plate.

To open the coconut (adults only!): With your biggest knife, chop the top off with several whacks, holding the bottom of the coconut with your hand. Do not miss. (Or, go to howtoopenacoconut.com for a more studied approach.)

Macadamia Nut Ice Cream

1 C Raw Macadamia Nuts (or Cashews or Almonds)
1 Thai Coconut (Water and Pulp, ask an adult to open this)
1 Vanilla Bean
1 C Filtered Water
Agave Nectar to taste (kids are best for this taste test)
Optional: 1/3 C Cacao Powder for Chocolate Ice Cream

Blend and put in your ice-cream maker.

Mama Louks Says: I just blend up the vanilla bean, pod, seeds and all. Some chefs remove the pod, but both ways are fine. It is a lot quicker and easier to toss in a vanilla bean, and I haven't noticed a difference in taste. David Wolfe's Web site, sunfood.com, has the best prices I have found for vanilla beans.

Banana Splits

Chocolate Sauce:
> See "Raw Chocolate" recipe. Instead of pouring the chocolate in molds, pour directly over your banana split.

> Banana
> Macadamia Nut Ice Cream
> Chopped Almonds (or try the Mesquite Walnuts or Pecans)
> Toppings: Almond Butter, Cacao Nibs, Berries, Raw Cereal, or even Chocolate Chip Cookie (see cookie recipes) crumbs on top.

Slice banana in half. Use ice-cream scooper to scoop out ice cream. Pour chocolate sauce over ice cream. Sprinkle with toppings of your choice.

Mama Louks Says: Doesn't just looking at this recipe inspire you to have an ice-cream party? The idea here is: Go for it! Don't limit yourself. Because I need to minimize my sugar, I leave out the banana and opt for a "chocolate sundae." However, these fats are not only good for you, they are essential for a balanced diet. No more dieting! With raw food, it is really difficult to overeat natural fats. Our bodies have natural stopping signals in place, and they will tell you loud and clear when you are done. Just listen.

Carob Balls

> 1 C Raw Almonds
> 8 Dates (seeds removed)
> 1 C Rah! Rah! Cereal (see recipe)
> 1 C Carob Chips

Chop the almonds until they are the size of small chunks in the food processor. Add the remaining ingredients in the food processor and grind up well.

"We served this at a party for my gymnastics team and they quickly disappeared. They were very yummy," Heather, age 10.

Mama Louks Says: We found this recipe blended up more easily in the food processor with the "S" blade. The carob chips are not technically raw, and you can buy the unsweetened or the sweetened variety. I will usually mix half and half for the kids.

Chocolate Chip Cookies

2 C Almond Flour
3 T Coconut Butter
1 C Dried, Shredded Coconut
8 Dates (Blend with Coconut Butter in blender and a little filtered water)
1/2 Vanilla Bean
Pinch of Sea Salt
2 C Cacao Beans
Maple Sugar to taste (kids love it with 1/4 cup, but skip it if you are diabetic or sugar sensitive)
1/2 C Maple Walnuts (or Pecans)
Delicious Option: 3 T of Dried Coconut

Day 1: Soak walnuts for 4 hours. Chop into small chunks (or ask an adult). Stir in 2 T of maple sugar, a pinch of salt (and optional: 1 tablespoon of mesquite powder). You might triple this batch. It makes a great stand-alone snack for the kids, and it is great on spinach or arugula salads. Spread onto a dehydrator sheet and dehydrate at 100 degrees overnight.

Day 2: Put all the ingredients in the mixer, mixing in the cacao chips and maple walnuts last. Press dough into cookie shape, small shapes for a class or large groups as they are quite filling, or Mrs. Field size. Eat as is or dehydrate at 105 degrees overnight or up to 16 hours. They make the house smell good, and start disappearing quickly. You might want to double, no triple, this recipe.

Day 3: Enjoy!

Mama Louks Says: The cacao bean does have trace amounts of caffeine, but it is also loaded with nutrients and protein. It is considered by some to be a super food.

Sunorganic.com makes great almond flour. You can also substitute sprout flour, but I never found it.

You might want to dry your own coconut, as the store bought varieties are pasteurized. Just grate in a food processor and dehydrate for 2 hours at 145 degrees and continue at 95 degrees for at least 12 hours.

Caramel Chews

1 C Raw Almonds, ground to powder

1 C Raw Cashews, ground to powder

1/8 C Flaxseeds, ground

1/8 C Agave Nectar or Maple Syrup

1 t Vanilla Extract

1 T Maca Powder

Combine ingredients in a food processor. Form into balls. Freeze or flatten and dehydrate 1 hour at 145 degrees, and 6 hours at 105 degrees.

Mint Chocolate Chip Cookies

1 C Raw Almonds, ground to powder

1 C Raw cashews, ground to powder

1/8 C Flaxseeds, ground to powder

1/3 C Chocolate Chips (vegan)

1/8 C Agave Nectar or Maple Syrup

1 t Peppermint Extract

Follow directions above.

Almond Butter Cookies

1 C Almonds (soaked 12 hours)
8 Dates, pitted
1 T Raw Almond Butter
1/4 C Unsweetened Carob Chips

Follow directions above, but save the carob chips. Flatten balls and decorate cookies with carob chips. Super simple!

Coconut Brownie Balls

4 C Almond Flour
3 C Coconut Flakes (dried at a low temperature, unsweetened, free of sulfites)
1 C Cacao Powder
1/2 C Maple Syrup
3 T Coconut Butter
1 T Vanilla Extract
1/2 t Sea Salt

Combine ingredients in a large bowl (use a stand mixer if you have one). Spoon dough into your hands and press into a 1 inch diameter ball. Dehydrate at 145 degrees for 2 hours, and then at 95 degrees for approximately 8 more hours or so ... if there are still any left.

Mama Louks Says: When Jeff takes these to his work, I get calls from his colleagues requesting the recipe. They are a hit with the kid's classmates.

Chocolate—Raw

1 C Cacao Powder (ground Cacao Beans)
2 T Coconut Butter
2 T Agave
Optional: 1/2 C Un-soaked Almonds (finely ground, or chunky if you prefer)
1/2 C Finely Chopped Dried Coconut
2 T Carob Powder
1 T Mesquite Powder or Maca Powder (super foods)
1 t Peppermint Extract
1/2 Vanilla Bean (inside only)
1/4 t Sea Salt

Blend ingredients in a blender (mixing in optional almond chunks last). Spoon chocolate into molds up to 1/2 inch deep. We like the small silicone muffin molds but any small food container will do. Refrigerate. Peel off molds or cut into squares when the chocolate is hard. Display on a cake plate on a cool Valentine's or Easter Day, or store in the refrigerator.

Mama Louks Says: Cacao Beans are rich in calcium. Carob is rich in magnesium. When these two minerals are combined, absorption increases!

We all know what the kids will be bombarded with at school on Halloween or Valentine's Day. I didn't want them feeling deprived, so we came up with this. The best part was making it together. Chocolate comes from the cacao bean, which, when eaten raw has a negligible amount of caffeine. It is considered by some to be a super food (See *Naked Chocolate* by David Wolfe and Shazzi).

On Valentine's Day, Charlotte's preschool class had a heart-shaped cookie decorating party—sugar central. Instead, I brought this chocolate in a heart shape, to decorate with almond butter, raspberries, and carob chips. Charlotte loved it. (I offered to bring chocolate and toppings in enough for the entire class, but they didn't seem to want to part with the sugar tradition. Perhaps next year they would take me up on it.)

Fudge Brownies
Easy fudge: try it—it's *amazing*!

1/2 C Raw Cashews
2 T Cacao Nibs
3 Dates
3 T Honey
1 C Organic Cacao Powder
1/8 t Sea Salt
1 t Cinnamon
1 C Coconut Shreds (Organic and Dehydrated)
2 T Maple Granules
3 t Vanilla Extract (or 1 t Mint Extract for Mint Fudge)
1 T Carob
1/2 C Filtered Water

Blend cashews in food processor with "S" blade. Mix with remaining ingredients, holding back 1/4 C water. Mix well. Add the 1/4 C of remaining water. Mix well. Pour into glass pie plate and freeze for at least 1 hour. Slice and serve.

Pie Crust

1/2 C Almonds (12 hour soaking is optional)
4 Dates (remove pits)
1 T Coconut Butter
1/4 t Sea Salt

Mix in a food processor with an "S" blade. Press into a glass pie plate. Press a second pie plate of the same size into the crust to improve the shape. Freeze (or dehydrate overnight).

Chocolate Mousse Pie

Pie Crust:
    See recipe, adding 1/4 C of Cacao Beans)

For the filling:
    5 Thai Coconuts (flesh only)
    1/4 C Agave Nectar
    2 C Pistachios and/or Macadamia Nuts
    3 T Carob Powder
    1/4 C Cacao Powder
    8 Dates, pitted
    1/4 Vanilla Bean
    2 T Mesquite Powder
    1 t Coconut Butter

Blend until thick and smooth, pour into pie crust. Garnish with cacao bits and mint leaves. Refrigerate 1 hour or so. Enjoy!

Mama Louks Says: When we make this mousse, the girls and I end up enjoying a coconut-water party with the leftover coconut water. Try it; it's delicious!

Malibu Mud Pie

Pie Crust:

See recipe, adding in the 1/4 C of Cacao Beans. Freeze for at least 5 minutes.

For filling:

1 C Coconut Water
1 C Coconut Meat
1 C Almond Powder
1 Vanilla Bean
2 T Agave
2 t Coconut Oil
3 Dates, pitted

Combine in a food processor with an "S" blade. Pour over pie crust and freeze for 1 hour

For Topping:

Chocolate-Raw: see recipe. Do not add any of the optional items
Optional: 1/2 C Mesquite Pecans
Chocolate-Raw, curled with a vegetable peeler
Almonds, finely chopped
Strawberries and Cream (see recipe)
Mint garnish

After blending filling ingredients, pour over frozen filling. Freeze. Remove from freezer 15 minutes before serving. Decorate with optional toppings.

"For my next birthday party, I want to serve bean burritos, cut cucumbers, fruit, Lemonaid ... and for my cake ... Malibu Mud Pie!!!" Hailey, age 8

Mama Louks Says: This is a favorite at birthday parties, and as an "ice cream sandwich," so delicious, and it is the *real thing*!

Peach Pie

Pie Crust
　See recipe

Filling:
　8 Really Ripe Peaches
　1 T Cinnamon
　1 t Psyllium Husk (optional)

Combine filling ingredients in a nonmetal bowl. Set bowl and pie crust separately in the dehydrator for 2 or 3 hours at 145 degrees. When ready to serve, spoon filling into pie crust and serve!

Mama Louks Says: Peaches, nectarines, apricots, and apples all work well in this recipe.

Easy Peach Pie

　Peaches or Nectarines

Slice fruit in half. Place slices on a dehydrator sheet. Dehydrate at 145 degrees for 3 hours. Enjoy warm! (Or freeze and eat through the winter)

Cream

　2 C Macadamia Nuts
　1/2 C Lemon Juice
　1/3 Vanilla Bean
　1/2 t Cinnamon, plus extra for decoration

Cherimoya Custard Cream Pie

Pie Crust:
See Chocolate Mousse Pie

For Filling:
6 Cherimoyas
Juice of 2 limes

Cream:
See recipe, substituting orange juice for lemon juice
Mint garnish

Prepare pie crust and put in the dehydrator at 145 degrees.

Prepare the top layer, the cream, by blending the macadamia nuts, orange juice, vanilla bean, and cinnamon. Refrigerate.

Skin and remove the seeds of the cherimoyas. Mix with lime juice. (I mash it all together, but it might look prettier if the cherimoyas remain sliced.) Put cherimoya mush into pie. Smooth cream on top. Refrigerate or eat immediately. Sprinkle pie (and plate) with cinnamon before serving. Garnish with mint.

Strawberry Shortcake

Rah! Rah! Cereal, dehydrated as bars.
Cream (See recipe)
Sliced Strawberries (whole raspberries or blueberries also work well)

Using a knife, spread the cream thickly over the cereal bars. Decorate with the berries of your choice.

Mama Louks Says: Try alternating decorative rows of blueberries and raspberries. This makes a festive dessert at Memorial Day or Fourth of July parties.

Easy Cheesecake

Filling:
  2 C Raw Cashews
  1 C Almond Mylk
  1 Heaping T Raw Honey
  Optional: 1/2 Vanilla Bean

Blend on high for one minute. Set aside in a bowl, save 3 T of mixture

Crust:
  1 C Mesquite Pecans (See recipe)
  3 T Cheesecake Mixture

Chop in a blender using the lowest setting until pecans are finely chopped. Press into a glass pie plate. Pour filling onto crust. Decorate (see below) and freeze. Remove from freezer 15 minutes before serving.

Mama Louks Says: An infinite amount of variations can be made out of this recipe. Our favorite is blending 1/2 of the filling mixture with 1/2 cup of blueberries, swirling the two mixtures together over the crust and letting the children decorate the cake, making a happy face with additional blueberries. Another variation is doing the same with strawberries. For Chocolate Cheesecake, blend 1/2 C of cacao into mixture and decorate with cacao sprinkles. For Pumpkin Cheesecake blend in 2 t of "pumpkin spice" and decorate with sprinkles of cinnamon. This cake gets finished off quickly by our guests. That said, although cashews provide a creamy consistency, according to Dr. Cousens, they have mycotoxins, so go easy on the cashews.

Chapter Seven:
What We Think—A Kid's Perspective (and Some of Our Favorite Vegan and Vegetarian Cooked Recipes)

Are you a Raw Kid? Well, we are not. Our parents are raw, but we (the kids) eat about 50 percent raw foods, because we also like sprouted breads and tortillas, spelt and buckwheat soba noodles, quinoa, vegetable and lentil soups, raw goat cheese (goat's milk is cleaner, lower in fat, and easier to digest than cow's milk) and black-bean burritos! Steamed artichoke, corn, and broccoli are often seen at our dinners. If we make quesadillas, we use sprouted grain tortillas and put lots of veggies in them, like zucchini, chard, spinach, or sprouts, and sometimes avocado.

Why Raw? Here some of our thoughts on it:

"I don't really like raw foods, but there are some foods I do like. My favorite raw foods are raw cookies, raw tomato soup, vegan tuna, humus, vegetarian sushi, Caesar Salad (without the croutons, because they aren't raw), 'Nerds,' and everyday fruits and veggies. Sometimes (when I'm in the mood for it) I'll eat carob balls and raw ice cream. I also like lemonade with agave for the replacement of sugar. Those are all my favorite raw foods.

"If you are making raw foods a bigger part of what you eat, to make it more appealing, just add salt. Just kidding! Try putting salad or other things on a piece of sprouted toast and then gradually transition to the veggies and raw crackers.

"My advice to kids that are at birthday parties and other junk food situations is to not make an issue of it, just say, 'No thank you.' If it is a long birthday party you can bring some snacks for yourself. If there is a piñata, then give away your candy.

"Eating raw helps me with my tennis, basketball, and surfing. (Well at least my mom says it helps me with my endurance.) I guess raw helps you to run faster. My tennis is getting stronger, and I hit the ball so hard I get blisters on my hands. I'm in an older group than I'm supposed to be in for basketball and I like to sprint down the court on fast breaks. Surfing I just started so I'm not so sure about what raw has to do with that. So raw food helps you run faster," Lauren, age 10.

"How I like raw food: when we first started eating raw food, I hated it. After a few weeks, I started loving the smoothies my mom made for me. Then I started making my own smoothies.

"Then my mom started making cookies. In the beginning, I didn't like them at all. Then I liked it a little bit, and then my mom started making a whole different type of cookie. First they were bad, then better, then good, then terrific.

"My parents think raw food is good for me because it still has all the nutrients in it and it's not processed or pasteurized. They don't want me eating sugary junk because the stuff that is in it has gone through heating and chemical processes and has pesticides, no fiber and is not natural.

"I like going to parties. I think it's okay My mom always has me eat a good meal before I go, so when I'm there I'm not hungry. Sometimes I bring my own food, but usually there are fruit and veggies there to munch on.

"My advice to kids whose families are thinking about eating more raw foods is to start out slowly and make your way there gradually.

"When I first tried coconut water, I only liked the first sip. The next day I liked 2 sips, and so on. Now I can drink a whole coconut. With the coconut, you have to get used to it.

"I want to get a gymnastics scholarship for college. I think raw food will help because it will give me the energy to run fast on vault and do the four-hour workouts," Heather, age 10.

"This is what I *don't* like about junk food and cooked foods: At school, my friends get sick sometimes and then I don't get to see them.

"This is what I *do* like about raw foods: They are very good for me and my mom makes them delishy (delicious).

"At parties, junk food is everywhere! Cake—ewe! Gross! Well, it tastes good, but do you know what is in it? Sugar, sugar, and more sugar! Ta-gross! It's not even real food! If you feel like trying it, tell yourself ten times, 'If food's junk-y, it's not for me!'

"Some great raw choices to eat instead are our Raw Chocolate, Coconut Brownie Balls, and our popsicles. I like Lemonaid and fresh-squeezed orange juice.

"I like cuddling and reading with my mom and preparing food with her, especially when it is Christmas. My mom is mostly raw, and that is very good for you. Now she feels much better and she's a much better mommy. When she used to have headaches, I couldn't play with her because she wasn't feeling well. That's why I like raw food," Hailey, age 7.

"Junk food is cake, licorice, candy, popcorn, chips, orange cheese, fruit roll-ups, (kid's) vitamins, candy bars, and all yucky gross stuff. If somebody has chocolate, just say, 'No thank you.' I don't eat chicken because cooking them is not nice, and I love horses.

"I like going to the farmer's market with my mommy because I love fruit and vegetables and tasting them. I like raw crackers with avocado and (sea) salt. I like raw hot chocolate with a little agave and making orange juice. Leaves! Ice popsicles! Passion fruit, pomegranate, peaches, pineapple, and 'shark bubblegum' (a.k.a. kale leaves)!" Charlotte Grace, age 4.

Kid's Pizza

Soft Spelt Bread Pizza Crust (see Spelt Crackers)
Organic Tomato Sauce
Raw Goat Cheese (grated)
Broccoli, Kale and/or Zucchini (lightly steamed or blanched)

Make your own pizza! Combine your favorite ingredients, and put in the dehydrator on high for 15 minutes.

Pupusas
Delicious zucchini quesadillas!

1 C Zucchini (grated)
1/4 C Onion (grated)
1 t Coconut Oil (and more for large frying pan)
1/2 t Herbamare
Sprouted Grain Tortillas (we like Ezekiel Tortillas)
Raw Goat Cheese (grated)
Optional: 1 t Horseradish

Step 1: Heat frying pan with coconut oil on high heat until coconut oil liquefies and covers skillet. Add onions and heat for 3 minutes. Change heat to medium and mix in zucchini, Herbamare, and optional horseradish. Cover lid and let sit for 3 minutes.

Step 2: Heat large frying pan on medium heat and cover with coconut oil. Lay a tortilla flat in pan, and cover half with cheese and the zucchini mixture. Cover and let stand for a few minutes. Next fold over 1/2 of tortilla to make a quesadilla and whoo-la!

Mama Louks Says: This recipe has been a hit with the entire extended family and birthday parties. A great quick substitute for the zucchini mixture is spinach, kale, chard, or collard greens added raw at Step 2. It will soften while the quesadillas are cooking. Jeff and I will occasionally enjoy these sans the cheese, with a boatload of greens in them.

Note: I use stainless-steel frying pans. Iron skillets are another good option. Avoid clad or nonstick frying pans. The kids know how to make these Pupusas, quesadillas, and burritos, and that when the pan has a good amount of coconut oil over it and then heated, it is much easier to clean later.

Black Bean Burritos

1 C Black Beans (soaked for 3 hours)
1/2 Onion (whole)
3 Garlic Cloves (whole)
2 1/4 C Filtered Water
1/4 C Kale or Chard
1 C Cooked Rice
Sliced Avocado
Raw Goat Cheese (grated)
Sprouted Grain Tortillas
Coconut Oil

Rinse beans well and simmer with onion, garlic cloves, and 2 C filtered water for 1/2 hour. Blend mixture in blender, adding kale, and 1/4 C filtered water.

Heat skillet and cover with coconut oil. Lay down a tortilla and add black-bean mixture and rice down the middle. Heat for a few minutes on medium heat and then add avocado slices. Roll up into a burrito. Enjoy!

Mama Louks Says: We eat salad every night. Sometime the girls choose to have their salad rolled up in their burritos or quesadillas just to change it up a bit.

Black Bean Soup
Easy to make, and everyone loves it!

1 C Black Beans, soaked for up to one day
3 C Filtered Water
4 Garlic Cloves
1 Onion
1 T Terragon, minced
1/2 t Salt
1/2 C Spinach (or Chard)

Boil ingredients (except spinach) 45 minutes. Remove garlic and onion. Add spinach and serve.

Mama Louks Says: If the kids pick out the greens, next time blend the greens with 1/4 C water, turn the heat off the soup, and quietly add the green liquid. Enjoy the sweet revenge—they will never know!

Lentil Soup

1 t Veggie Soup Starter
2 Tomatoes
1 Garlic Clove
1 1/2 C Filtered Water
2 C Fresh Lentils, sprouted
2 T Onion or Scallions, finely chopped
2 T Cilantro or Basil, finely chopped
1 C Spinach (or Kale, Chard or Collard Greens)
1 Medium Zucchini, sliced
1 Carrot, sliced
1/2 t Avage
1 t Herbamere

Blend soup starter, tomatoes, garlic clove, and water. Pour mixture into a stainless-steel sauce pan. Add lentils and onion and bring to a boil. Boil for 30 minutes. Add remaining ingredients and heat for 3 more minutes. Serves 6.

Mama Louks Says: Lentil sprouts are 26 percent protein and can be eaten raw.

White Bean Soup

2 C White Beans, soaked in water overnight
1 t Veggie Soup Starter
2 Tomatoes
2 C Filtered Water
2 Garlic Cloves
1/2 Onion, finely chopped
1 Stock of Celery, finely chopped
2 Stocks of Kale, finely chopped
Salt to taste
1 Rosemary Sprig, stem removed and finely chopped

Blend soup starter, tomatoes, filtered water, and garlic cloves. Pour into a sauce pan and add beans, onion, celery, and salt. Simmer for 45 minutes. Add kale and rosemary and heat 2 more minutes. Serves 6.

Squash and Garbanzo Bean Soup

2 C Yellow Squash (or Zucchini)
1 C Filtered Water
3 Carrots
1/2 C Sprouted Garbanzo Beans (or Sprouted Mung Beans or Sprouted Lentils)
2 T Onion, sliced
1/4 C Basil
1/4 C Cilantro
2 Garlic Cloves
2 T Flaxseed Oil (or Olive Oil)

Steam squash, beans, and onion for 2 minutes in 1 cup of filtered water. Let stand for 2 minutes. Pour water, squash, carrot, beans, and onion in blender, adding basil, cilantro, and garlic. Blend until smooth. Mix in oil just before serving. Serves 3 adults.

Mama Louks Says: If you'd prefer this soup with a tomato base, you can use the previous recipe, substituting the white beans for peeled and chopped squash and garbanzo beans. Toss in some basil leaves from your herb garden if you have it! This recipe is also a big hit without the garbanzon beans!

Broccoli Soup

2C Filtered Water
3C Broccoli, chopped
3 Garlic Cloves
1/4C Onion, chopped
1/4C Basil, chopped
1/4C Cilantro, chopped
1t Sea Salt
1t Extra Virgin Olive oil

Steam broccoli, garlic and onion for 3 minutes. Blend with hot water, in blender, adding in remaining ingredients.

Split Pea Soup

1C Split Peas
1 Large Tomato, finely chopped
3C Filtered Water
4 Garlic Cloves, finely chopped
1/4C Onion, finely chopped
1/4C Cilantro, finely chopped
1 Large Carrot, chopped
2 Medium Zucchini, chopped
2 Celery Stalks, finely chopped

Rinse peas. Soak peas for 30 minutes or so in 3 cups of water. Add tomato, garlic, onion and cilantro and cook for 40 minutes. Add in carrot, zucchini and celery and cook for 3 more minutes.

Easy Quiche

1 Dozen Eggs
1/2 t Sea Salt
1/2 C Zucchini
1/2 C Spinach
1/4 C Basil
1/4 C Onion
1/2 C Raw Goat Cheese, grated

Preheat oven to 350 degrees. Whisk eggs and salt together. Set aside. Combine zucchini, spinach, basil, and onion in a food processor with an "S" blade. Add plants and cheese to egg mixture. Pour into a glass pan and put in the oven for 20 minutes. Serve hot.

Mama Louks Says: I add this and the following recipe because their redeeming qualities are that the kids consume more plants and the recipes don't use cooked oils.

French Fries

6 Potatoes, large
1 T Sea Salt, mixed with 2 cups of filtered water
Optional: Raw Goat Cheese, grated

Heat oven to 350 degrees. Slice potatoes into French-fry shapes (which is easy to do with a mandolin). Soak fries for 5 minutes in 2 cups of filtered water and sea salt. Drain water in a sieve and let stand for 5 minutes. Put potatoes in a glass pan and bake for 20 minutes. Remove from heat, sprinkle optional cheese if you'd like, and serve immediately.

Mama Louks Says: Imagine ... French Fries without cooked oil (and the kids love it!)

Chapter Eight: Fermented Foods

Fermented foods with live cultures and probiotics have many health benefits. They are rich in enzymes which aid digestion and introduce "good" bacteria into the digestive tract (or re-introduce good bacteria after using antibiotics). I found them balancing and helpful in overcoming my sugar addiction.

My first foray into fermented foods was with kefir, as I read that the animal protein in the dairy milk is predigested by the healthy flora (good bacteria) of the kefir grains, and therefore a healthier animal protein. I bought the kefir grains from gemcultures.com. For kefir cultures to grow, they need to be in dairy milk. If I put the grains in almond mylk every day, the grains would soon die out. So I would alternate making kefir with almond mylk and raw goat milk, adding the almond kefir to our smoothie. (I prefer goat's milk to cow's milk as it is a cleaner animal and the milk is lower in fat.) I got use to it, and grew to really love it, but Jeff didn't like the sour taste. Ultimately, we were still drinking dairy residue and kefir making became a part-time job. Fermenting coconut has been much simpler, dairy free, and tastes great. The fermented veggies has taken some getting use to (I have never been a sauerkraut lover). In the winter, when our garden offers less variety, we will enjoy a small amount our stash of fermented vegies with our main meal of the day.

Coconut Yogurt

Water and Flesh of One Coconut
1 Packet of Kefir Starter (or 1 T Bio-K Vegetarian Probiotics)

Open the coconut. Remove flesh of the coconut. Blend the coconut and water until creamy, approximately 30 seconds. Add Kefir Starter or Bio-K, blend on the lowest setting for 5 seconds. Pour in a jar, secure lid, and store in a dark place for about 8 hours. Refrigerate yogurt for one week and your Coconut Yogurt is ready! It can be stored in the refrigerator for up to 6 months. After a few months the yogurt will become more firm and tart, with a more intense flavor, almost like cheese.

For the next batch of Coconut Yogurt, simply blend coconut water and flesh with a spoonful of the previous batch, as long as the batch is at least a week old or longer.

Mama Louks Says: A proper method for removing the flesh of the coconut can be found at howtoopenacoconut.com. It is much more thoughtful and elaborate (and a bit more time intensive) approach than my machete maneuver (see page 63).

I prefer to use the Kefir Starter because the ingredients are cleaner. Kefir Starter may be purchased through Body Ecology at bodyecology.com, 800-511-2660.

Coconut Fizz

Water from One Coconut
Kefir Starter Packet (or 1 T Bio-K Vegetarian Probiotics)

Pour ingredients into a jar. Secure cap and shake gently. Leave in a dark place for about 8 hours. Refrigerate 1 week. Enjoy, or leave in refrigerator for up to 6 months. The longer it is refrigerated, the stronger the ferment and fizz.

For the next 6 successive batches, use a spoonful of the previous batch for a culture starter.

Fermented Veggies

Veggies: Cabbage, Fennel, Onion, Garlic, Carrots, etc
Filtered Water
Lemon Juice (from 1/2 lemon)
Optional: Culture Starter Packet from Body Ecology

In a food processor using an "S" Blade, chop up veggies. Put one cup full of veggies in the blender and liquefy to create brine, and then add in optional Culture Starter. Pack veggies into a mason jar. Pour brine over veggies and then lemon juice. Fill remainder with water, secure lid, and let stand on the counter for 3-5 days. Enjoy, or refrigerate for up to 6 months.

Mama Louks Says: The lactobacillus in the culture is said to be a beneficial bacteria to improve digestion, support a strong immune system, and help stop sugar cravings.

Chapter Nine:
Raw Household Cleaners

No more chemicals in our homes! Here are some really simple recipes, and they work better and are much less expensive than the chemicals!

How many of us have grown up in families that have been indoctrinated with television commercials with smiling actresses promoting new (chemical) cleaning products? We then began buying these new cleansers, pleased with their results, but not thinking of the side effects.

Cleaning and cosmetic products are two types of pollution that are under-regulated and un-policed. Where cosmetics are required to list their ingredients, cleaning products are not required to list ingredients, and they usually contain toxic poisons! Statistically, if Americans are not putting much thought into the quality of their processed-food products, we are putting even less thought into the quality of our cleaning products.

The ultimate place to get your cleaning products is your own kitchen, and these recipes get the job done. Plus, when we use reusable bottles, we eliminate a tremendous amount of waste. The recipes below are simple, inexpensive, and gentle to the environment. My favorite is Raw Raid, and you will be amazed at its effectiveness.

If you choose to purchase cleaners, Gaiam has an excellent catalog, *Real Goods* www.realgoods.com, 800-919-2400. *Real Goods* is a great resource guide for products that support a sustainable world, including cleaning products that are biodegradable and nontoxic. The guide points out that we are often using *hazardous chemicals* to clean our house. To quote the writing in the guide, "The average household contains 3 to 25 gallons of toxic materials—and ironically, most of these are in the products we use to get our home 'clean.' Common cleaners are made with a staggering array of suspected carcinogens, ingredients that break down into even more toxic compounds and chemicals so dangerous they're associated with Superfund sites."

Also, an informative and motivating read on green cleaning and cleaning products is by Deirdre Imus, *Green This!* Deirdre shares the lowdown about the hazardous ingredients in typical American household (and school) cleaners such as chlorine and petroleum distillates, dioxin and triclosan, ammonia and formaldehyde, phenols, butyl cellosolve, and alkylphenolics. If you see these ingredients, run.

Some of the recipes below call for *organic* vinegar. Keep in mind, the cost of organic vinegar is still much less than store-bought cleansers.

If you have rosemary in the back yard, here's a great, low-costing, easy way to freshen up the house. Boil rosemary for 5 minutes. Strain water and use in one of the recipes below, especially the floor cleaner. Your home will have the clean scent of fresh rosemary. Have pine leaves? Soak the pine leaves in vinegar for 5 days, and you have Pine Solve.

Finally, some of the recipes include the option of using organic essential oils, either as air fresheners or for their antibacterial qualities. Oregano, as well as basil, thyme, and clove are especially antibacterial. Our favorites are rosewood, grapefruit, lemongrass, tangerine, rosemary and eucalyptus, cinnamon and spruce, as well as rosemary and clove are winning combinations to use around the holidays. Combine your favorites!

Dish Cleaner

Warm Water
1/4 C Organic Distilled Vinegar
4 Drops of (your favorite) Essential Oil

Fill sink or a large bowl with warm water. Instead of reaching for the petroleum, laurel-sulfate-laden dishwashing detergent, grab your vinegar and essential oil, and enjoy the aromatherapy while you do the dishes. (Note: This works beautifully with raw foods, not with cooked oils and bacteria from meat and dairy. Sorry!)

All Purpose Cleaner

2 C Warm Water
1/4 C Organic Distilled White Vinegar
1 T Lemon Juice
Optional: 10 Drops of (your favorite) Organic Essential Oils.

Combine

Mama Louks Says: If you are looking for an all-purpose cleaner without vinegar, there are many new, competitively priced nontoxic cleaners on the market now. Some of our favorites are Meyer's (also check out their stainless steel cleaner), Aubrey Organics Earth Aware, Seventh Generation (also check out their citrus carpet cleaner), Ecover, Planet, and Bi-O-Kleen. These brands also make nonhazardous, automatic dishwashing detergents. However, vinegar is a great astringent. It even works well on toilets Just pour 1/2 cup into the tank and scrub.

Countertop Cleaner
Good for most countertops

3 C Warm Water
1/2 C Organic Distilled White Vinegar
1 T Lemon Juice
Optional: 10 drops of your favorite Organic Essential Oils

Combine

Mama Louks Says: We use this on granite countertops. However, avoid using vinegar on marble or limestone. I shudder to think of what we used to clean our kitchen countertops with—toxins.

Floor Cleaner: Tile and Stone

1 Gallon of Water
1/2 C Organic Distilled White Vinegar
Juice of 1 Lemon
Optional: 20 drops of your favorite Organic Essential Oils

Combine. For wax finish and wood floors, use vinegar only. Do not use vinegar on marble.

Window Cleaner

3 C Warm Water
1/2 C Organic Distilled White Vinegar

A quick method to apply this is to apply cleaner with a cloth and then squeegee. (Did I say quick? It takes significantly less time using this recipe than the leading brand.)

Laundry Detergent

3 Chinese Soap Nuts (good for 2 or 3 loads) in a small mesh bag

Mama Louks Says: "Maggie's Soap Nuts" are great. The soap nuts grow on trees. By purchasing soap nuts rather than our typical laundry detergent, we supports trees and avoid bringing more toxic chemicals into the environment. Also, for a great fabric softener, add a splash of distilled vinegar into the rinse cycle. For deep stains, try diluted lemon juice and sunshine.

Easy Blender Cleaning

2 C Warm Water
1/4 C Lemon Juice (or 1/2 C Baking Soda)

Blend!

Cleaning for that Cutting Board!
Especially wood cutting boards

Sprinkle salt on the board
Rub the cut side of a lemon over the board
Rinse with hot water (dry wood boards immediately)

If you are wondering if your board needs cleaning, just smell it. A smelly board is not only bad for your health; it makes the food taste horrible! Please clean your cutting boards regularly. For extra tough jobs, try soaking the board in vinegar.

Rust Cleaner

1 t Salt
1/2 t Lemon Juice (or Vinegar)

Using an old toothbrush, scrub away. Rinse with warm water. For tough stains, including moldy grout or shower drains, try adding baking soda and make a paste. Apply it to the area, cover with a towel, and leave it on for several hours before rinsing with warm water.

Look out for rust, especially on anything that touches food. Rust most often shows up in the kitchen on anything aluminum that was washed and not dried right away. (I shudder to think of those rusty aluminum cookie cutters I found in my drawer) First off, avoid putting aluminum in contact with food. Second, if it won't come off, like those aluminum cookie cutters, toss it.

Drain-flow

1/2 C Baking Soda
1 C Organic Vinegar
Boiling Water

Using a funnel, pour the baking soda down the drain. Follow with the vinegar. Wait a few minutes and follow with boiling water. The septic tank will thank you.

Furniture Polish

1/2 C Organic Olive Oil
3 T Lemon Juice
10 Drops of (your favorite) Essential Oils

Pour ingredients into a spray bottle and shake well.

Mama Louks Says: If you have oils other than olive oil that you need to move off your shelf, this might be a good opportunity to make room for fresh oils. You might want to do a spot check first, to make sure it doesn't change the wood's color.

To clean outdoor furniture mix 1/2 C organic vinegar, 1 C water, and 5 drops of Tea Tree Essential Oil (or 2 t of Tea Tree Oil). Spray over furniture. Let sit for 10 minutes then wipe off. For cushions, let spray dry. Test on wood to make sure finish doesn't peel off.

Raw Raid

Organic Vinegar in a Spray Bottle
Boiling Water

Spray vinegar on the ants when they come marching in, and lay them flat in their tracks (oops—is that vegan? Well, I think Raid does the same thing, but with highly toxic carcinogens). Boiling water poured down the ant hill will finish off the rest of them.

Mama Louks Says: If this sounds too harsh, here is some interesting information. Ants thrive in dry, inert soil, as opposed to rich, loamy, organic soil. So, if you want to eliminate ants the holistic way, join me, and start composting!

Section Two: Lifestyle

Chapter Ten:
Our Family's Story, Continued,
and Practical Questions
and Answers

Nutrient Pitfalls

Like a savings account endowed with daily deposits, children flourish with consistent, nutrient-rich meals. These meals are intrinsically more valuable than all the stuff (toys, clothes, electronics, etc.) we give them.

But what are nutrient-rich meals? Our family has also experienced the tragic pitfalls of a teenager who decided to step out from the family's traditionally omnivorous diet to be a vegetarian, yet not knowing or learning how to be a successful vegetarian, becoming, instead, a junk-food vegetarian. This can lead to serious health problems.

Healthy vegetarian, vegan, and raw-foods diets need to avoid the pitfalls and be especially mindful of the following 4 considerations: minerals, Vitamin D and Vitamin B12 sources, and lowering fat content.

Minerals are abundant in leaves, and you'll read more about how we can more easily assimilate minerals in leaves in the "Light Filled Leaves" section. Also, the first recipe in this book is the most important. It's a delicious, green, "Super Power" breakfast smoothie (see recipe), rich in minerals.

Incidentally, magnesium, one of the minerals Americans are most deficient in, is most abundant in the cacao bean (*Naked Chocolate* by David Wolfe and Shazzi), so check out our chocolate desserts.

Another important consideration for a mineral-rich diet is that organically grown foods are mineral-rich sources, while conventionally grown foods are not as rich in minerals.

Finally, the *water* we drink can be a source of minerals. The water our ancestors drank used to be a mineral source, and now with our modern filtering systems, although they remove pollutants, they also remove many of the minerals. (Read more on buying organic and water in subsequent chapters.)

Our best source of vitamin D is ultraviolet B rays: sunshine! The next most common source of vitamin D is synthetically made and added to milk. So encourage the kids to turn off the television set and computer games and go outside and play! (If they don't go out in the sun much, start with 15 minutes to build up a base.) Those of us who are working long hours or living north of the 50th parallel (where they only have 6 months a year to increase their vitamin D storage) will want to take careful consideration of their vitamin D sources. Sunscreen has its place, and there are some great chemical-free sunscreens out on the market today (see chapter on Chemical Free, Often Organic Cosmetics), however, consider that when we slather on the sunscreens, not only do sunscreens usually contain endocrine disrupting chemicals, we also can be blocking those vitamin D supplying, UVB rays.

Dairy foods are naturally rich in vitamin D and could be a vitamin D source, however, when dairy products are pasteurized, this heat process destroys the natural Vitamin D. In pasteurized milk, synthetic vitamin D is required by law to be added back into this milk. Hmm …

Our Louks children get some of their vitamin D from raw goat cheese, but mostly from sunshine. We disconnected the television when the girls were little, way before our raw journey began. Now I realize we had an added bonus; we disengaged ourselves from the onslaught of advertising. This was probably instrumental in stepping out of the ingrained way of thinking our culture has toward cooking and processing everything that goes into our mouths! Yes, we occasionally enjoy movies, but even with those, I have my own small protest.

It started when we were watching *Dreamer.* Dakota Fanning, the jockey, and the trainer take a minute break from the practicing for the upcoming horse race. Out comes the Krispy Kreme donut box, the box is opened, and the donuts are enjoyed with smiles and laughter. The movie producers probably increased revenues, and Krispy Kreme enjoyed a commensurate increase in sales … but is this something I want to raise my children on? Think about it: by turning the tube off, not only will they get more vitamin D, it will make it a lot easier for the kids to move away from junk food.

The third and perhaps most important nutrient vegetarian and vegan/raw families want to address is their source of vitamin B12. Recent studies have shown small to significant B12 deficiencies in 80 percent of adult, raw-food eaters (and 35 percent of meat eaters have significant B12 deficiencies as well as a host of other deficiencies). I hear termites and insects are great sources of B12; our prehistoric ancestors ate them, and they are big in other cultures, but—yuck! When it comes to my children, I am not going to mess around; our solution is to give them a sublingual, organic and vegetarian B12 vitamin every other day.

In regards to fat intake, one of the biggest pitfalls of raw foods is a tendency to get the majority of our calories from processed oils and also avocados, nuts, and seeds, versus lower-calorie fruits and vegetables (which can contain around 5 percent and 10 percent fat calories, respectively (see nutridiary.com for exact amounts). Please keep in mind, the path to optimal health is a moderate-fat, raw diet that avoids processed oils and consists of predominately whole fruits and vegetables. In between these meals, snack on cucumber, celery, purple cabbage, etc.

So if you are more than a casual reader and are planning on changing your foods choices toward a vegetarian, vegan, or raw diet, you might want to consider turning off the tube, but definitely give careful attention to your daily mineral sources, Vitamins D and B12 sources, and fat intake.

Real Nutrients

Back to the migraines ... here I was, up against this wall, praying and searching for answers. I felt I should start somewhere, so I decided to take vitamins. Soon I realized that, for me, the vitamins were a mistake. I think there is a lot more we have yet to understand about how we assimilate the nutrients in our (dead) vitamins. But, more importantly, I was sensing the need to discover the larger picture—what is food, really?

Food is much more than calories, vitamins, and chemical processes. Although dietetic analysis and scientific research point to the constituent elements of food such as vitamins, vitamins do not come close to representing true nourishment. Food is not about decompounding food or mistaking the individual parts for the qualitative experience.

As I am growing in my understanding, I see food as a qualitative experience that can strengthen my spirituality and honor our interconnectedness. I began to think about the beauty in the mundane and how nourishment relates to kindness, respect, and gratitude for those who help to grow and prepare our food; about honor and respect for our environment (including the honey bee and the earthworm), including humane and fair trade along the path to the table; about honoring the seasons that usher these foods in and connecting with people and the interrelatedness we exist in. All this contributes to nutritional food, with stronger life force energy, moving at higher vibrations (than "denatured" food); a gift meant to lift us higher in our experience of divine love. Food brings us together; it is much more than a nutrient source.

Our body-mind-spirit needs far more to find deep satisfaction. To me, food became a manifestation of divine love, bringing us higher in our experience of Love's extraordinary creativity packaged to sustain and delight us. Food is not Love, but one of the many varied *expressions* of Love. Ultimately, our satisfaction doesn't come from food. Satisfaction comes from our personal and individual assimilation of Love. This comes from experiencing the bigger picture of our true nature.

It might sound strange to say, "Come over for dinner and have some love." And I wonder if it will take a paradigm shift before we truly understand what I'll term as the "spiritual design" of our bodies. From this perspective, perhaps we will better understand how we assimilate our food.

I also wonder, when we are eating living foods, if the amount of nutrients in plants is as important as what we *don't* eat. In other words, pure, living foods don't have some sort of supernatural healing powers. We align ourselves with supremely natural healing power when we endorse and buy locally, love and respect nature and animals, and honor our planet.

For example, giving up aspartame or saccharin, refined sugar or cooked oils, white flour or other processed foods can result in a greater level of health—much more than choosing goji berries over blueberries. My healing lay in what I was willing to give up. When I avoided food other than pure and living foods, I felt better and found healing and a greater level of health.

And it is all connected. If we are going to progress as a global community, our purchases must be seen as what we are supporting; essentially as our *vote*. It also helps considerably in developing a healthier relationship with our planet and changing our course toward global warming. I think it is this *purifying* process that rejuvenates us. *It lies in what we are willing to give up.*

Unfortunately, this is a concept that doesn't have much scientific support. (It hasn't been studied in detail because it does not offer much financial profit. For example, there is not nearly as much research on how to avoid cancer as the billions of dollars spent on how to find a (pharmaceutical) cure for cancer. There is a lot more profit in finding a pharmaceutical cure. However, there is some research pointing to how love and gratitude create more alkaline environments, decreasing cancer cells (see "Alkaline versus Acidic"). Another body of research that points towards the purifying process is Masaru Emoto's photographs of water crystals. Featured in the film, *What the Bleep Do We Know!?* and his inspiring children's book, *The Hidden Messages of Water*, Masaru shares photographs of beautiful water crystals when water has been in a loving, thankful environment. (Note: the human body is over 75 percent water.) These two areas of research help to connect the dots for us between this purifying spiritual process and the resulting manifestation of physical health.

So where do our best sources of nutrients come from? What I learned through my vitamin research was that vitamins (and diet formulas) are a *mega*-billion-dollar industry. Big money is spent promoting these products, and we tend to buy what is advertised. Vitamins are often cooked and filled with sugar and other chemically altered or synthetic ingredients. When we heat fruits and veggies, they loose up to 80 percent of the nutrients. If you do take supplements, make sure they are organic, high quality, and naturally derived.

On the other hand, organic fruits and vegetables, although natural and loaded with vital nutrients, don't get the limelight, so to speak, like vitamins often do. Although less expensive, conventional produce typically has 50 percent less minerals and nutrients than they did in the 1950s. And who wants traces of pesticides and chemical fertilizers in their food? They are poisons! Plus, when we purchase conventional produce, we are supporting and endorsing a practice that is damaging our precious earth. In season, organic is the way to go. (Read more about "Local, Organic, and Seasonal" toward the end of this book.) Ripe, freshly picked, organic fruits and vegetables are loaded with nutrients, including vitamins and minerals.

Adieu Sugar Blues

Along with the vitamins I ordered came a book (*The Schwarzbien Principle* by Dr. Diana Schwarzbien). This book touted the benefits of losing weight. I thought, "Great, another diet book." But in the small print I read something about "fatigue," so I picked it up and started reading.

The book convinced me to give up sugar (good-bye Ben and Jerry's!) and white flour (Ciao pasta! Sayonara sushi! Adieu sourdough bread!) I never thought I was addicted to these white, powdery substances. You have no idea until you take them away. I started "climbing the wall," especially around that time of the month.

Another book, *Sugar Blues* by William Dufty, gives a fascinating history of sugar. William shares that it wasn't until the twelfth and thirteenth centuries that the Crusaders brought sugar from the Middle East to Europe. Sugar became the hot item, kind of like the billion-dollar pharmaceutical industry is today. Spain, then England, began growing sugarcane in the West Indies to meet the rapidly growing demand. (This sugar demand also funded the Royal British Navy so that Britain became the most powerful nation of that era.) Workers were needed to cut the sugarcane, so Europe began trading sugar (or sugar fermented into rum) for *slaves* in Africa, and brought them to the West Indies. Thus became the beginning of the slave trade that eventually came to America. Slaves—all because of the demand for sugar!

Sugar is addictive. If rats are given a choice between (highly addictive) cocaine and sugar (sucrose or saccharin), they will most often select sugar (*Intense Sweetness Surpasses Cocaine Reward*, Magalie Lenior). Tracking the growth of sugar from the fourteenth century, William shows how every successive century, Europeans and Americans have substantially increased their sugar consumption. He points out that there is an increase in diabetes in direct proportion to the amount of sugar imported to that country.

Nowadays, sugar is in almost every food and beverage commercial we see. Our increase in sugar consumption is alarming, especially considering the fact that there are no nutrients or fiber in refined sugar. Sugarcane is refined, heated, and chemically altered so much that the only thing left in sugar is calories. In turn, diabetes (types one and two), which was almost unheard of before refined sugar, is steadily increasing in our society. Seven percent of U.S. adolescents have a prediabetic condition, impaired fasting glucose. (2008, National Diabetes Fact Sheet, U.S. Department of Health and Human Services, Centers for Disease Control and Prevention)

Looking at the history of sugar, it makes me think of the analogy of the frog in hot water. If the frog is placed in hot water, it will immediately jump out. However, if it is placed in cool water and the water is gradually heated to boiling, the frog doesn't jump out. We are like the frog, not realizing the water is getting hotter, or rather, not realizing we are swimming in junk foods.

What can we do? First, we can develop an awareness of our environment. Just like the drug pushers and beer commercials, I think we need to explain to our children the motives of the sugar pushers. The more we eat sugar, the stronger our addiction, and the more money is to be made by companies. Think about it: this is capitalism. If someone wants to sell a food product, they can cheaply sweeten it with sugar. Even worse, they could sweeten it with high-fructose corn syrup, a highly processed derivative of corn. Either way, they will probably increase their sales volume.

Even our *dental floss* often has a sugar coating! This is really brilliant because floss is not a food, so it is not required to list the type of sweetener. I'll guess the cheapest sweetener available is used: high-fructose corn syrup. (In fact, most major sodas have switched from refined sugar to corn syrup: empty calories, just like sugar, only cheaper.) Or it could have been saccharin, but I'd hope that the dental-floss company would be required to have the label that the other thousands of saccharin food products have: "Warning: Saccharin is a known carcinogen."

Soda experiment: Take a can of sugary, caffeine-loaded soda. Pour it in a bowl over rusty nails or dirty coins. Watch what America's favorite beverages do to the metal. Water anyone?

White flour is just as denatured as refined sugar except that we add synthetic vitamins back into the flour (after all the nutrients and fiber are processed out) and then call it "enriched." Refined carbohydrates convert to sugar quickly, which explains our culture's current starch addiction to pizza, pasta, bread, etc.

It all starts with awareness. We have friends whose children eat a good amount of sugar and white flour and they get sick a lot (sound familiar?). When they go to see a doctor, the doctors recommended taking the children's tonsils out (doctors, is it too much to suggest a junk-food-free diet?). I asked one friend how his child was doing after the surgery, and the answer was telling, "I think she has recovered well, she is able to eat ice cream again!" Hmm.

After learning how harmful sugar really was, the next step for our family was to kick the sugar habit. We wanted to be healthy and wanted the kids to have a high level of health. Parents, it is worth it. To encourage principled, healthy food choices is a deep expression of love and wanting only the best for our children. Personally, for me, it was a tough few months kicking the sugar and flour habits, probably even more difficult than it was for the kids because my habit had years on them. Plus I still wasn't feeling that great. Fortunately, I remembered that stash of raw books I had received from Don. He was an angel in my life. To think I almost tossed them out the year before.

Raw Cuisine

The books started me on a great adventure exploring better alternatives and recipes (see the references in the back of this book). Some recipes tasted great, some just took a little getting use to, and some really didn't taste good. They weren't kid tested. True, it really comes down to individual preferences, but if it doesn't taste good, children quickly lose interest. Improving on these recipes became the foundation for the recipes in this book: foods that are really good for us and that also taste great to the entire family.

These books brought out some fascinating points. Cooked grains have been challenging for me to eliminate, and our children are still eating them. The problem with eating large quantities of cooked grains (and animal proteins) is that their digestion creates an acid environment and, in order to get back into balance, calcium is pulled from our bones. (Note the unusually high level of osteoporosis in our country's population, which is raised on dairy, meat, and grains). Also, the mycotoxins in these grains and cooked food compromise our optimum health.

In his book, *Rainbow Green Live Food Cuisine*, Dr. Gabriel Cousens makes a strong case for avoiding mycotoxins found in, among other foods, flours and stored grains. When you see his pictures of what mycotoxins do to blood, you might want to steer clear of them, too. He suggests eating the freshest vegetables, fruits, nuts, and seeds, and sprouted, uncooked, unstored original grains. He points out how humans had thrived for five million years before the introduction of grains (pg. 19). Imagine if, instead of clearing land to plant grains, we planted fruit trees (think avocados, especially in less-developed countries). Couldn't an acre of fruit trees feed more people than an acre of grain? (With fewer chemicals, less fuel burned, and more absorbed CO_2; it would be an example of permaculture—permanent agriculture supporting permanent culture.) So I thought I'd test his theory, but could I replace these time-honored staples on which I had been raised?

I was far from being "raw." I didn't even know it was possible to survive on raw food. I had eliminated sugar and white flour. I was feeling a little better. Yet, I still had migraines that made me wonder if my head was going to explode.

Next step: we went to a raw restaurant. I took Jeff, my husband to "Juliano's Raw" in Santa Monica. We had a date night every Saturday night. It was my break every week—my big night out on the town. For the past few years, Jeff's favorite restaurant (and now the children's, too) offers local, vegetarian fare: bland, cooked, and boring. Don't get me wrong, I ate fairly healthy, with salads every night, but this was over-the-top just—bland! So I have this great idea: instead of going to our usual place, let's check out this raw restaurant.

As we were approaching the restaurant, I had this sinking, regretful feeling in my stomach. Jeff was hungry. I wondered if we'd have to go to another restaurant afterwards to get satisfied.

We sat down and were offered a very long menu. Reading the menu was like getting an education on global warming. I found out there was more I could do to help stop global warming than to start carpooling or change my light bulbs. (Compact fluorescent bulbs are laced with *mercury*. On that path, if we don't dispose of them correctly, we'll have zillions of these bulbs ending up in our landfills and ultimately more mercury in our waterways.) We read (a truly inconvenient truth on) how we could save our planet from global warming by avoiding animal products and eating organic, local produce. (Note: livestock emit 37 percent of anthropogenic methane. This methane is 21 (to 23) times the global warming potential of CO_2. The global production of meat is expected to double from 229 million tons in 99-01 to 465 tons in 2050. The planet's current total area of grazing is 26 percent of ice free terrestrial surface ... can we allow this to double? Source: "Livestock's Long Shadow", 2006, a LEAD publication [Livestock, Environment and Development], recently published by FAO [the UN Food and Agriculture Organization]).

From this perspective, modifying our diet can do a lot more for our planet than driving a Prius! Plus there is more. Guess who is the largest marine predator? The cow! "More than half the fish taken from the sea is rendered into fish meal and fed to domestic livestock." Puffins are starving in the North Sea because we feed their food to livestock. "Sheep and pigs have replaced the shark and the sea lion as the dominant predators in the ocean and domestic house cats are eating more fish than all the world's seals combined. The oceans have been plundered to the point that 90 percent of fish have been removed from their ecosystems and this very moment there are over 65,000 miles of long lines set in the Pacific Ocean alone and there are tens of thousands of fishing vessels scouring the seas in a rapacious quest to scoop up everything that swims or crawls" (e-mail from Paul Watson, previous director of the Sierra Club, 2003-2006).

This sheds a whole new light on what tree we need to bark up if we are going to reverse global warming. I recently read the mayor of London recently enacted a tax of ten thousand dollars on all SUVs. This is good, but what if the tax was placed on meat? Well, yes, the mayor would probably quickly fall out of popular favor and be removed from office, but just think of what it would mean for our environment.

Years ago, I threw up my arms in despair with the public school system in disbelief when one daughter came home from school telling me that cow farts are a bigger cause of global warming than gasoline. I found myself biting my lip. I'm finding out it's the decomposing manure as well as the flatulency, but now I could see her point. I also hear that some public school's nutrition classes are now teaching the kids to eat more fruits and vegetables and limit eating meat to once a week. Bravo!

Back to the menu ... I continued reading about the enormous amount of gasoline used at the many levels of meat production, the hormones, and pesticides fed to our livestock (conventionally grown feed for livestock accounts for about 80 percent of our agricultural land), and the animals' alarmingly cruel environment, and about the pesticides and fertilizers killing our environment and ocean life. It took us an hour to sit and read the menu.

We decide to order the sampler plate, at the recommendation of our very-tattooed waitress. (Okay, I don't get out all that often, with four children and all, but I have never seen a woman so tatted. Snake tattoos cover her chest and arms. I try not to stare.)

True, we are famished by the time the food arrives, but I tell you honestly, and surprisingly, it was the best food I had ever tried in my life! The food was full of flavor, interesting, and delicious. A whole new realm of culinary possibilities opened up for me that day.

Pure Raw

I had been reading (in my raw book collection from Don) about all these amazing turnarounds from chronic diseases: cancer, heart disease, diabetes, chronic fatigue, and even migraines—all from "going raw." Well, after I discovered how delicious the raw food could be, I decided to just do it—I went raw.

People ask me if it was really hard to eat only raw food. To be honest, I really had to have one of those "not my will, but Thy will" conversations. I had to be willing to give up my personal attachments, and when I did, *amazing* things started happening. The migraines stopped, and my energy soared. My focus and vision is stronger, and it feels so good to be back in the driver's seat in my life. I thank God every day for my health, family, for giving us this rich, diverse, beautiful planet to take care of, and for guiding me how to take care of myself.

The Cosmetic Racket

By telling us to stay out of the sun to avoid premature aging, the cosmetic industry has created a desperately pale-faced market eager to cover imperfections. Our culture is obsessed with appearances; we get fat sucked out and silicone and Botox put in. We put such an importance on how we look that we don't stop to think of the health risks these procedures induce.

To make the lotions and potions more marketable, dyes and chemicals are added. Petroleum products are used for their consistency and parabens and xanthan gum are used to lengthen the shelf life. Sunscreens are loaded with chemicals and over-the-counter drugs, which we religiously slather on our children when they step foot outside.

I soon became more aware as to what cleaning and cosmetic products were in my environment. (Cleaning products are loaded with poisons. Have you ever checked to read what is in your dishwashing detergent?) I stopped applying anything that wasn't 100 percent natural and mostly organic on my skin. Confession: I was a top director/saleswoman for the best-selling cosmetic brand in America for sixteen years. I have dry skin, and I love to lube on the lotion. However, researchers are finding that skin, our largest organ, is absorbing these cosmetic ingredients, including petrolatum, mineral oil, lauryl sulfate, parabens and urea (preservatives), and other synthetic and chemical ingredients, into our system. We are drinking up chemicals. Toxin central!

I have had an ongoing dialogue with my (ex)company about the importance of all natural ingredients in cosmetics, and they say their toxic ingredients are just part of the industry standards. They point out that mineral oils and parabens are a staple in most major cosmetic companies and are even standard use in medicines. "But," I respond, "medicines are usually not used morning and night, day in and day out!" Well, the company is not budging, for now. It is a big company—perhaps a dinosaur now—and the conversation with them continues.

Nine months into my raw path, I had the courage to take some blood tests. I tested out with elevated levels of heavy metals, like aluminum, lead, mercury, nickel, and tungsten. I have no known history of specific heavy-metal exposure, except for cosmetics, cooking with Teflon pans, and previously eating a weekly serving of tuna and salmon. So, I am suspicious of cosmetics, especially lip products. If you have young daughters, I encourage you to take a close look at their "play" lip glosses and glitter make-up, and toss them out if they have chemicals in them.

I am also suspicious of the harsh cleansers used in our home and the chlorine and fluoride in our water. These harsh chemicals cause dryness and break down the skin tissue so that it is not as effective as a protective barrier against bacteria (and heavy metals?).

Since I began this raw adventure. I have been experimenting with organic and chemical-free cleansers and cosmetics, and there are some great alternatives, even chemical-free waterproof sunscreens. Chapter 19, at the end of this book, offers a list of favorite store-bought, chemical-free cosmetics and natural-care products. Also, I have included some natural (and raw, just for fun!) recipes for cleaning our homes that are easy to prepare in Chapter 8.

Animal Proteins and *The China Study*

So I wonder if these toxins were just overloading my system. Who really knows, but I read a compelling book recently released, *The China Study* by Colin Campbell. He shows with his thirty-five years of high-profile research how toxins tend to stay in our bodies when we eat animal proteins (meat and dairy). He shows conclusive evidence that toxins flow through the body more easily when we are eating plant-based foods. Colin makes a fascinating distinction between the "diseases of the affluent" (*diet*-related diseases such as heart disease, cancer, Alzheimer's, diabetes, etc.) and diseases of the impoverished (parasites, cholera, other diseases relating to unclean water, etc.). He shows how these diseases of the affluent are not as much influenced by genes as the family and cultural dietetic and lifestyle traditions passed down to the children.

After sharing a myriad of researches, Dr. Campbell concludes that a plant-based diet can offer more far-reaching benefits than medicines or surgeries, even that, "advanced heart disease, relatively advanced cancers of certain types, diabetes ... can be reversed" (pg 22, 23). This book, along with the "Eating" video (see references) and the most recent medical research linking cancer and meat, make a convincing case for giving up animal proteins.

Light-filled Leaves

I was reading that it was important to eat leaves. Looking back at this past year, I can see how following this lead and making them a primary part of my diet was the key in cleansing and changing my course. I ate collard greens, cabbage, carrot tops, radish tops, arugula, bok choy, fennel, amaranth, alfalfa, comfrey, grape leaves, and watercress. Then I ate the lettuces: Romaine, Miner's, butterhead, loose-leaf, chicory, frisee (the list of edible leaves is endless). I then moved on to my current favorites: hearty, mineral-rich weeds like dandelion, wheatgrass, and my favorite, *nettles*.

Did I just lose you? These leaves are one of the most nutrient-dense foods around. However, there is a secret on how to eat these leaves and absorb their rich source of magnesium, amino acids, iron, chlorophyll, calcium, folic acid, etc. The secret is in *blending* the leaves into *green smoothies*. Over the course of several months, my body adapted and my digestive strength and absorption improved, perhaps from an increase in hydrochloric acid and enzymes. Go easy on the spinach, arugula, kale, lamb's quarters, sorrel, Swiss chard, beet tops, poke, New Zealand spinach, amaranth greens, and parsley. They are rich in nutrients, but, in addition to alkaloids, they also contain high levels of oxalic acid. So if you or yours are prone to kidney stones or gallstones, you might want to skip spinach. (growingtaste.com/oxalic acid.shtml) If you can stomach it, like my friends down at the Optimum Health Institute in San Diego, drink small amounts of wheatgrass daily.

Author and raw foodist Victoria Boutenko discovered this, but she found she just couldn't stomach raw leaves. Brilliantly, she developed green smoothies; blending the leaves with fruit. And believe it or not, they start to taste great. (Even sweet, but remember, it takes two weeks for our taste buds to regenerate, so stay with it.) Her compact disk and books (see rawfamily.com) make a great case for having more leaves in our diet. She compares their fibers to sponges, mopping up toxins as they go (and suggests blending rather than juicing or fasting to cleanse). Think about how strong a moose, horse, bull, or zebra are from eating greens. The chimpanzee, who is closest to our DNA, eats primarily greens and fruits.

Because of the various alkaloids in leaves, it is important for us to vary our selections, just like the deer, which eat many different varieties of leaves.

My favorite leaves to blend are nettles. Interestingly, nettles have a different self-preservation system and do not have any alkaloids. They sting! So use gloves when putting nettles into your blender. Once blended, they won't sting you.

The most important recipes in this book are the "Super Green Power Smoothie" and "Green Soup" because they contain blended leaves. Also, these recipes, along with the cheesecake, will be a big hit with the more senior members of your family (dentures and all). When you blend up your leaves, you rupture their cells and the nutrients are easier to assimilate. It might take a while for your body to adjust to assimilating these leaves. Try small bunches of new leaves at first and build up gradually. For Jeff and me, it took a few months to adjust. Now if we miss a few days of green blending when we are traveling, we really start *craving* Green Smoothies!

Fresh Fruits

Good news: whole fruit is also important! Good, because most children love fruit, and it is the ultimate fast food—taking less time to prepare than the drive thru! The children like fruits because they are loaded with natural sugars. We now keep lots of seasonal produce in our kitchen, and it rapidly disappears. Every week, our trip to the farmer's market brings a new discovery. There seems to be an endless variety of fruits. Our family can go through a big box of tangerines in four days. Have you ever tried passion fruit? It tastes better than Sour Skittles. Moro (blood) oranges attract the children like flies, and then there is the cantaloupe with lime.

We rarely drink fruit juice anymore. Not only is it hard on kid's teeth, fruit juice, like other refined sugar and starches lacking fiber, have a high glycemic load. Simply put, the glycemic load indicates the level of sugar that goes into the blood when the food is eaten. A high glycemic load means the body converts the food to sugar quickly, and it can be hard on the digestive system to handle so much sugar, especially for the diabetic or sugar-sensitive person like me. This can also wreck havoc on the immune system. So, generally, as a family, we avoid juice. Fruit is to juice like sugarcane is to sugar. They are worlds apart.

Once your fruit is opened, it starts to lose nutrients, so eat them soon after you open them. Eat whole, freshly cut fruits as much as possible.

Some of the lowest glycemic fruits are berries (we love blueberries, raspberries, blackberries, and strawberries). Citrus, apples, and pears are also fairly low glycemic fruits.

In the recipes included in this book, fruit (for example date or banana) is my personal favorite sweetener. It is a whole food. Other sweeteners used are dried fruit, date granules, stevia (in herb form), agave nectar, or yacon syrup. Although not whole foods, they are also good, raw options the children like. I do sometimes include organic maple granules or organic maple syrup as an alternative. I personally avoid it, but it sometimes is a key ingredient in making the food kid edible. I figure, whereas sugarcane tends to be hard on the land, the more maple trees we encourage, the better off our permaculture, and the better off our planet. Every purchase, whether of conventionally grown sugarcane or maple sugar, encourages pesticide-ridden cane or—trees!

In addition, we also give the kids raw honey in their almond mylk (they love it) and on their almond-butter sandwiches. The kids also like the honey comb, and all of it is edible. They sometime chew on it for a while, collecting it in their mouths as gum. (However, the wax looses its flavor rather quickly.)

With all honeybee products, especially bee pollen and royal jelly, be sure to introduce it in tiny amounts, to make sure your family members don't have an allergic reaction to it. And wait to introduce honey to babies until they are two years old.

I don't consider the food that comes from the honeybee's hive, the honey and pollen, to be animal products, but flower products. In climates with snowy winters, when flowers are hard to come by, bees rely more on their stockpile of honey to make it through the winter. However, here in California, where bees collect honey year round, they will produce more honey than they can eat. If the hive gets full, the bees are forced to leave their hive, and make a new hive. In other words, eating the surplus of the bee's honey is not necessarily a detriment to the bee. However, watch out for brands that take all the honey from the hive and leave the bees with an alternative sugar. Look for bee-friendly practices.

Forgotten Fats

Along with leaves and fruits, it is important to eat a small amount of fats. True, we are bombarded at every turn in our culture with advertisements for low-fat foods and drinks, as if fats are unhealthy. Well, it is time to reprogram. It is the *processed, cooked* fats we want to avoid. The essential sources of fat come from whole, raw, plant-based foods. When the fats are natural, raw, and plant-based (versus long chain saturated fats found in animal proteins), they are good for us. (Even essential.) True, obesity is our country's most serious health problem; it is not from eating raw fats from whole plant foods.

In our recipes, you'll see fat-based foods like avocado, olives, coconut, flax, chia, and hemp seeds, and other seeds and nuts. These uncooked fats are a *vital* part of our diet, and they are difficult to overeat. According to the Nutrient Database for Standard Reference, nal.usda.gov, avocados contain the 18 essential amino acids (proteins) and essential fatty acids (EFAs) including Omega 3 and 6, and no dietary cholesterol. (As a side note, did you know that dietary cholesterol comes from animals alone?)

However, go easy on the fats. Too much fat is a pitfall in a raw diet. Lighten up on the salad dressing, and go heavy on the salads, soups, and smoothies; munch on whole foods with minimal fats often (cucumber, celery, purple cabbage, etc.).

Protein

It is a common question: where do you get your protein? It is also a big concern for dietitians in America, who often encourage 30-50 percent of our diet to be protein. Interestingly, like fruit, protein levels in breast milk vary between 1–5 percent, depending on the needs of the child. Fruits mimic this protein level, and vegetables have roughly double the protein level of breast milk. This level drops when it is cooked and denatured. Unfortunately, when we think of protein, we too often link a need for animal based foods (beef, chicken and fish range between 20-30 percent protein). Ultimately, it is not the protein, but the amino acids in the protein that our body needs. Surprisingly, adequate protein is achievable through a balance of (blended) leafy vegetables, sprouts, seeds, nuts, and super foods. Check out our breakfast "Super Power Smoothies," afternoon "Lemon Chia Seed Drink" and evening "Chocolate Mylk" with cacao beans and maca and mesquite powders. But the most potent source of amino acids (and minerals) comes from *blending up leaves every morning* in that powerful Vita-mix Blender; blending makes the amino acids and other nutrients more digestible.

A high-protein lunch might include "Strawberry Crackers" spread with hemp-seed butter and topped with blueberries. A high-protein dinner might be the Pesto Pizzas on sprouted spelt with sprouted sunflower seed, "Cheeze," or Tabouli with sprouted quinoa. You'll find, with a little ingenuity, raw food can include protein-packed meals.

Here are my most successful, high-protein foods for the children: "Super (not quite green) Power Smoothies" with bee pollen, sandwiches with hemp seed and almond butter, "Chocolate Mylk," "Vegan Tuna" with sprouts, "Kid's Salad" (loaded with hemp or sesame seeds), and most of the desserts. If the children have bread, hopefully it is without flour, instead using sprouted, organic grains (more protein).

Cooked plant food is reported to have half the protein of raw plant food. Raw fruit is 5 percent (of calories) protein, raw vegetables and leaves (go spinach—31 percent!) are 10-30 percent protein, sprouts and nuts are 10-25 percent protein, seeds (hemp, flax, sunflower, and pumpkin) can be up to 33 percent protein. Seaweeds range from 12 up to 38 percent protein and super foods (bee pollen, algae, cacao beans, spirulina, and chlorella) can be up to 65 or 70 percent protein. (Note: see *The New Whole Foods Encyclopedia* by Rebecca Wood, 1999, Penguin Books.) So maximize your protein levels and think again about cooking your food. Warm it if necessary (up to one hundred and five degrees), but next time, don't cook it. (Note: especially with your children, always rinse your sprouts well before eating.)

Also, *organic* grains and seeds have significantly higher levels of protein (*Secrets of the Soil*, Peter Tompkins and Christopher Bird, Harper and Row Pub, 1989, pg 28) than conventionally grown grains and seeds. So doesn't it make sense that organically grown produce would also have higher protein levels as well?

I used to feel the need for a good amount of meat, cheese, and dairy in my diet. I found that once I eliminated refined sugars and simple starches (junk food) from my diet, I didn't feel I needed as much animal protein (especially meat) to balance out the sugars. Perhaps when we are eating these simple carbohydrates (sugars), our bodies might be asking for more animal protein, and vice versa. When we are eating more animal proteins, then we tend to crave more sugars (including alcohol—alcoholic beverages are fermented sugars).

Lewis and Clark's Corps of Discovery subsisted on primarily an animal-protein diet when they were exploring the west. It was interesting to read that with their meat-based diet, the big highlight of the day was their rum (fermented, refined sugar), and the result was boils and other physical problems. At any rate, with a pure, raw/living foods diet, the concern turns away from protein and sugars (carbohydrates) toward whole foods, leafy veggies (leaves), and fruits—and you will find delicious recipes that support this balance in this book.

With my recent blood test, I was curious as to what results would be found after nine months with this raw, vegan diet. I tested out "excellent" on my level of proteins (and everything else: folic acid, calcium, iron, pH balance—except B12).

So as you move into this diet, remember to include a good amount of proteins: blended leaves every morning, sprouts, (sprouted) seeds, and super foods.

Alkaline versus Acidic

Here's some food for thought: in 1931, Otto Warburg, in his research for the cause and cure of cancer, was given a Nobel Prize. He researched healthy cells and cell respiration and found that an alkaline environment resulted in healthier cells and a stronger immune system. Fermented sugar created a more acidic environment and gave a lack of oxygen to the cells.

How do we create a less acidic environment? Here is a synopsis: calcium, magnesium, silica, and iron are alkalizing minerals. These minerals are found abundantly in organic, raw, plant-based foods. Phosphorus, sulfur, and chlorine are minerals that are found in more acid-forming foods (see below). In a neutral pH or slightly alkaline environment, the good (healthy) cells eat the bad (cancer) cells. In an acidic environment, the bad cells flourish. At any given time, we all have these bad cells. However, when our cells aren't healthy (too acidic) the bad cells take over, and our immune system is weakened.

It has now been found that our diet, as well as our spiritual, mental, and emotional states, affects our pH level. Alcohol is highly acidifying. Also highly acidic is meat, refined sugar, flour, most grains, nuts, some seeds, cooked and processed foods (alkalizing properties were reduced or removed), soda water, soft drinks, coffee, medicine, and toxins.

Back to my TV soap box: think of the most recent commercial you saw for a pharmaceutical drug. Whether the drug was recommended to address high cholesterol, osteoporosis, cancer, diabetes, or migraines, it suggests that these conditions are diseases that can get fixed by taking a certain drug. What if we take a different perspective? What if we take the position that these are not diseases (and even that there really is no disease). What if we look at these problems as the *result* of an acidic and generally unhealthy environment? Could it be that the root cause of these maladies is consistently poor food choices and/or negative spiritual/emotional choices over time?

The most alkalizing foods are leaves. Vegetables are mostly alkalizing. Fruits, for the most part, are either neutral or slightly alkalizing. Interestingly, anger and hatred, negative thinking, and a lack of oxygen are related to a more acidic environment (I picture how I feel when I'm yelling at the kids). On the other hand, love, forgiveness, patience, and compassion can make one more balanced or alkaline.

How this relates to a living diet: gratitude for the gift of fruits, herbs, and seeds is healthy. Leafy greens and vegetables best support this alkaline/acid balance. Ripe fruits, contrary to what I thought, once digested, tend to be slightly alkaline or neutral. Citrus fruits are the most alkalizing fruit, and the lemon/chia seed drink is a nice neutralizing drink (see recipe). The recipes in this book are geared to support a slightly alkaline balance. Most importantly, our thought behind our food choices and life choices impact our level of health.

Junk Food Parties and the Writing on the Wall

Now, with such a big turnaround in health, I started to think there is really something *huge* about this diet and way of life. I am also enjoying the sunshine more and taking more time to breathe deeply and enjoy the moment. (Daily exercise, prayer, and deep relaxation are vital and have long been part of our practice.) Jeff, noticing a big difference, went raw soon after me, and is sold. So here's the biggest issue: if Jeff and I, as parents, are feeling great with this new diet, what about our children? At least one of our children goes to a junk-food party every week, where they serve pizza, chips, juice boxes or soda, cake, and ice cream (followed by a piñata). If I'm exaggerating, it's not by much. At school, they are barraged by candy grams, bake sales, lemonade stands, and my favorite—donuts! (New York has now passed a law preventing trans-fats from being served in restaurants.) *Trans-fats come from cooking fats that become unstable when heated. (So when/if you use cooking oil—use the highly stable coconut oil, also known as coconut butter.)* Oh, yeah, did I mention the school cupcake birthday parties, and all the holidays: Halloween, Thanksgiving, Hanukah, Christmas, Valentine's, Easter—all great junk-food opportunities.

We wonder why 19 percent of *our children* are overweight! Type 2 diabetes, once considered an adult disease, is increasingly being diagnosed in children. (Since when were children diabetic?) Antidepressant medication prescriptions for children are rising by about ten percent annually, and for preschoolers, these prescriptions are skyrocketing (Delate, Thomas, Ph.D., 2004, Psychiatric Services). The medical evidence on childhood health statistics is mounting. The writing is on the wall.

Purple Cabbage and "Just Limit Their Options!"

We decided to transition our children toward a healthier diet during a family vacation. We saw it as our chance to get off the track—the junk food track. The plan was to eliminate sugar and white flour and transition our children to a more whole, living-foods diet. We cleaned out all the cupboards and emptied the refrigerator (I highly recommend this, it makes life much easier) and started fresh.

Now, if children have to choose between junk food and whole food, be it the choice between cake and an apple, even if their body is craving an apple, they will more often reach for the cake. It is that sugar addiction! In order for us to move the children into a healthier diet, we had to stop supporting the addiction, stop supplying the junk. We began to feel empowered with the responsibility to be parents and only stock the shelves with good food.

I have a girlfriend who was recognized by the State of California for top performance in supporting the "No Child Left Behind Act." She worked in an inner-city school where most of the children were on an aid program that gave them free lunches at the school cafeteria. It was often the best meal they had all day; however, it was filled with highly processed foods. The cafeteria was mandated to have one whole fruit on their tray. Do you know what happened? They filled up on all the other food, and every day, my friend saw all this delicious fruit dumped into the trash. It is really important for us as parents to make sure we just put healthy options on our children's plates (and cut up the larger fruits).

When I bring whole food into our girls' classrooms and there are no other options, the children *devour* it. On Halloween Day, as a "Harvest Festival" alternative, I brought in pumpkin seeds (see "Rah! Rah! Cereal") with cut apple and pomegranates, and nothing was left—not even the pomegranate *seeds*! Also, for a birthday party, I came armed with "Chocolate Chip Cookies" (yes, raw, and full of nutrients, see recipe) and tangerines. I also had a head of purple cabbage, really my lunch, I presented to them first, more as a joke. They collectively devoured the cabbage (my lunch was decimated), and then moved on to finish even the last morsels of the raw cookies and tangerines. But here's the kicker: if pizza or cupcakes were around, they would have never tried the cabbage, pumpkin seeds, and perhaps even the raw, healthy cookies. As Jeff encourages, "Just limit their options."

Anunda: Raw and Rollerblading at Sixty

While we were on a summer vacation, we met Anunda. Anunda has a little restaurant in the back of the "Chapter One Bookstore" in Sun Valley, Idaho. Back in the early sixties, when he first found out about the raw diet, Anunda went raw by mostly eating fruit, so he has been a whole foods/raw eater for over forty years. He's now over sixty years young, currently planning to ride his bike this spring from Idaho to Arizona and then ride over for a visit here in California. He has a reputation in town for being one of the best mogul skiers. (Not many people over sixty ski like that.) We really enjoyed talking with him and mentioned to him that we were planning on driving to Yellowstone National Park, a three-hundred-mile drive. He replied that last year he rollerbladed from Sun Valley, Idaho, to Yellowstone. And it took him only two days. He said he also rollerbladed to Oregon one time and said he was going so fast a police officer pulled him over. (He was clocked going down a grade at fifty-two miles per hour. The officer thought he might like to know how fast he was going. I hope he was wearing his helmet.) Anunda said his muscles never really get sore, and he thought because of his diet, his body didn't produce lactic acid. He also said his knees are virtually the same as they were when he was in his twenties.

Not only did Anunda keep us well supplied with great food on our vacation, he is also an inspiration. In the back of this book, you'll read some thoughts from our children. They talk of running fast. It might come from Anunda's inspirational example of what is possible.

The Community Connection

Mealtime is now much more than just a meal for us. The kitchen has moved back to the center of our family life, as we prepare whole foods together. Preparing food together has become an enriching, attachment-building, bonding time. As they say, "people support what they help to create," and the girls enjoy the food even more when they have played a part in planting, growing, selecting, or preparing of the meal.

Eating together as a family (versus eating alone) supports the children, as well as me, in making balanced food choices. It is an ideal time to connect with each other. The food seems to taste better, too.

On the flip side, the more time I spend with the girls, the more living foods they eat. They don't eat all my foods, but they get curious and tend to experiment and enjoy more whole, raw foods when we are together.

Here in the United States, traditional cuisines have evolved and morphed into our standard American fare (think burgers, pizza, soda, ice cream, coffee, beer, and wine). These new "traditions," however hard on the environment and our health, are at most of our social gatherings. Then there is the economic factor: the lower the income, the more refined sugar and oil consumed. It's much less expensive to throw a "junk food" birthday party than one with a freshly prepared meal. However, affluence doesn't necessarily mean healthier diets. Affluent Americans are often just as prone to eat "ignorantly," with "financial success and nutritional failure" (Barbara Kingsolver, *Animal, Vegetable, Miracle*, pg 129). Hmm—alarming bedfellows: affluence and ignorance.

There are strong trends in all social climes away from freshly prepared or "home cooked" meals, toward fast foods and bringing processed foods into our homes. Another trend is that we are spending less and less of our net incomes on our food. Quality food has not been valued as much in our culture as in the past.

So here we have an evolution of the standard American diet into something we as parents are seriously questioning. These trends can make social situations for any conscious eater difficult. For our family, social situations will expose and highlight different values, and at social gatherings, we sometimes struggle to find common ground.

Hopefully, with this exposure, we are raising the children with a conscious awareness of the environmental as well as economic factors that have moved our culture away from eating quality foods. Rather than jumping into the food at these gatherings, we want our children to understand the dynamics of this standard American diet—eat the good and leave the bad. This way, they can still connect with our community and its many culinary celebrations

Some friends and family have distanced themselves from us. And, as we grow, we change, and sometimes we move in different directions. However, our changes in our diet have opened the window to tremendous social blessings. Eating primarily whole foods has sparked new, deep, enriching friendships. With these new friendships, we are fostering new culinary traditions, and it feels good.

Sharing meals with friends and other families who also value whole foods has increased our connection with healthier foods. Potlucks are a great way to give and receive new, alternative ideas. Raw food get-togethers have been a great springboard for developing new friendships and strengthening others. Plus, the food can be inspiringly delicious.

Practical Questions and Answers

Question: Do you use *all* organic produce? I think that they carry pretty much everything in the organic variety at my local health store, but it is kind of expensive (Nancy, Newport Beach, CA).

Response: I buy all organic. Bottom line: I won't support pesticides and chemicals put into our environment. I have been thinking a lot about this lately. The cost of fresh organic produce has its costs, but we are paying even more on the back end for health care (especially for the farmers and field workers) and environmental damage when we buy conventionally grown produce.

I wonder if new, kosher laws were written into the Bible, given today's farming practices, what they would say? It is a moral thing for me (the moral act supports my spiritual strength) and a values thing (most of Americans live in two hundred fifty thousand dollar-plus homes, but can't afford to buy organic? Can't afford to save our environment?). Instead, we pour ammonia down our drains and slather our children with chemical sunscreens. I hear Americans spend 8-9 percent of our income on food. Europeans, on the other hand, place more value on the quality of their food, spending up to 35 percent of their income on food.

So, organic has the light shining most for me. I think our underlying spirituality is strengthened supporting our highest sense of right. This is my inner dialog. (See the following chapter for a more in-depth discussion on this topic.)

Question: One more thought: I wondered if you carry your commitment to organic over to clothing. I read somewhere that buying one organic cotton t-shirt will save two pounds of pesticide from being sprayed. Where can you find cute, organic, cotton clothes?

Response: Wow, you are amazing. NationalGreenPages.org. Also, a gal here in Pacific Palisades has recently put together Greenopia.com, which is now offering green phone books for major metropolises. Pantagonia was a forerunner in commitment to organic cotton as well as Timberland and Canadian Mountain Equipment Co-op. Earth Creation (earthcreations.net) has stylish options for the whole family. Gap, Nike, Levi, and Garnet Hill Catalog have some organic options the girls like. Also, Whole Foods is expanding their clothing line. Hemptations in Santa Monica has a great line of hemp clothing ("cotton uses 25 percent of all pesticides and hemp doesn't need pesticides" vitalhemp.com). Pharmaca Intragrative Pharmacy right here in Pacific Palisades has a few lines of casual, organic cotton and bamboo clothes for women (I especially like "Under the Canopy"). Whole Foods is starting to devote a part of an aisle to organic clothing. Gaiamliving.com has organic-cotton bras (sans the underwire). Secondhand clothing stores are the next step for nonimpact lifestyle. The girls and I are enjoying the hunt. We have made some great finds.

By the way, the store in LA that has the most raw foods is Erewhon on La Brea and Beverly (on Beverly two blocks east) near the Grove. I found it through Greenopia.

Question: How do you handle the whole birthday thing at your kids' schools? (Wendy, Pasadena, CA)

Response: This is a tough question. In our family, we talk a lot about the fact that all families are different and have different faiths, values, and rules. Our kids know our rule: lots of great food and no refined sugar or white flour. You will find the rules that you see as the most loving, balanced, and that work best for your family. Fortunately, we have a broad base of friends from different ethnic backgrounds: Jewish kosher, Indian, Romanian, Chinese, vegetarian, healthy eaters, and families who eat a lot of junk food. They are exposed to all of it and hopefully come back and appreciate the *luxury* of being able to have healthy food choices available. These are valuable learning experiences for them. If they can handle the sugar pushers now, they should be able to handle the drug pushers and inundation of beer commercials later.

One reason we see a lot of junk food in our culture is because we, as parents, are busy, on the run, and usually grab what is easiest and often, what is most advertised. To me, grabbing some raw foods on the run (usually fruit or crunchy veggies, nature's fast food!) doesn't take more time. Rather, it takes more planning and a bit more prep work, but who am I to judge what someone else feeds her children? The best we can do is be a role model for better choices, and I often find these junk-food families appreciate these pure, simple, fresh, and healthy ideas.

If we are going to set boundaries to junk food, we as parents need to really communicate with our kids about it and be willing to have conflict. Most parents, me included, don't want conflict. (But in result, we let them eat whatever they want.) I will never be able to control the incredible amount of junk food my kids are exposed to daily. All I can do is support them in establishing a healthy constitution. The first three months might be really tough, but I found it was worth it. For us, when the kids figured out we weren't bending, and their taste buds acclimated (I hear our taste buds regenerate every two weeks), they adjusted.

Three of our girls were at a public school and there is a growing awareness of the need to address these issues, not just for our own children, but for all children. I suggest meeting with the governing board of the school. Write a letter to the school and ask the principal to put you on the agenda (see my letter in the Appendix). The *LA Times* had a supportive article in September, "Sorry Cupcake, You Are No Longer Welcome," which stated the childhood statistics and reported how Texas and the Orange County Alison Viejo School District opted out. Instead of cupcakes, this school district celebrates birthdays with a song, a special book, and small gifts (like pencils)—and it is still really fun for the kids. (They might even appreciate the sugar relief.) Many school districts are rewriting policies to ban unhealthy snacks. I think it is only a matter of time until all do. One day, perhaps we will look back at the junk food at schools, and say remember when. Like we do now about how doctors used to recommend smoking to pregnant women in the 1950s. Remember, it was only until 2006 that they allowed soft-drink machines at (California) schools.

If you are not up to taking on the school district, which I still wonder if I am myself, explain to the teacher how you feel. Hailey's teacher was kind enough to now keep some Lara Bars (raw) on hand for these occasions. The private school our preschooler attends has gone above and beyond in accommodating my requests. Most importantly, I think the girls, especially the older ones, don't want to make a big deal of it. For the most part, they know all families have different foods they eat, and they just say "no thank you" when offered junk food. I try my best to make sure they have yummy food choices so they hopefully aren't tempted. (And that's the inspiration behind this book: great foods they enjoy, so they are fulfilled and not left feeling deprived.)

At Thanksgiving, each child had a class Thanksgiving party. For the older girls, it was mostly Domino's Pizza. For the younger girls, it was a step up: Kentucky Fried Chicken. I brought salads. The girls all ate my salad and fruit, but at Charlotte's preschool, the reaction was particularly interesting.

I was busy preparing for my first raw Thanksgiving, and realized I was late for Charlotte's Thanksgiving party. I was nominated to bring the water, specifically plastic bottles of water. Not wanting to support the landfills any more than I can help (Americans throw away 2.5 million plastic bottles every hour [Waste Facts and Figures, 2008, Clean Air Council]), and not liking the taste of plastic water that much (there is a difference), I quickly filled two clean glass carafes and packed paper cups. I made a few "Apple Sandwiches" (see recipe) and halved a few passion fruits. At the celebration, Charlotte had her special plate. The other moms were fascinated. Several (four) asked to try a bit from her plate. I sensed many of the moms left that day just a little more conscious of what choices we offer our children and how simple and *nonimpact* it can be.

They also got to try our "Pumpkin Pie." I used the recipe in *Raw Foods/Real People*. It's *amazing*. It doesn't have pumpkin in it, rather carrot juice and pumpkin spice with maple-covered pumpkin seeds on top. It is one of the best recipes I have used. It was a hit (and a great Thanksgiving Day treat), and I think some of these dishes really open our thought as to what is really possible with raw food. So, if you bring in special food for your child, bring extra. The interest is there and it is a great opportunity to share what you are doing.

Question: We have had a hard time the last two years with AYSO soccer, where each family alternates bringing snacks, often juice, candy, or fruit by the foot, or crackers with all the hydrogenated oils. Would you just tell your kids "no way?" What would you bring when it was your week? (Linda, Malibu, CA)

Response: "Just say no!"

Hailey played on a soccer team for a short period. On our day, I washed and then cut up a big bag of oranges. Another day, we cut up a big watermelon. The kids loved it.

Juice is overrated. Water is so much better for the kids. As I think I mentioned earlier, juice is to fruit as refined sugar is to sugarcane. My kids know how we feel about this, and I always have water and whole fruit available for them. That is my job.

Question: Then there are the holidays: here comes Valentine's Day—chocolate time! What about Easter and the egg hunts? Do your kids trick-or-treat? What about Thanksgiving—that's definitely a meal-centered holiday. Same with Christmas and New Years. And, what do you say to the relatives when they say, "You're only eating raw food?" (Nancy, Newport Beach, CA)

Response: So often we see our culinary traditions have evolved into junk-food fests! They are cheaper and take minimal time to prepare, and because of the sugar, our culture likes it.

If you are willing to take the path less traveled, wait until you try the "Chocolate—Raw" recipe. Your family and friends will get to experience the ultimate culinary delights. *Luxury* at Valentine's Day and Easter takes on a whole new meaning. The girls love it. It is a luxury to be able to eat this way.

That said, there will be challenges with this path. My mother-in-law had a hard time when we were at a restaurant and didn't eat the cake on her eightieth birthday. I don't think she is able to understand where we are coming from. I don't blame her, and she got over it.

This experience got me thinking about when Jesus sent his seventy disciples out to preach, teach, and heal. He told them to eat what is set before them. These disciples were Jews who during that day had a strict litany of dietary requirements. They were going into many different types of homes, including those of Samaritans.

If I am invited into someone's home, and they have prepared a special meal, I don't want to offend them or reject their offering. I had the opportunity to meet my new neighbors, Toby and Dick. They are an octogenarian couple who have offered their expertise at planting fruit trees. She swims every day, even in the freezing ocean water, and he runs on a daily basis (wouldn't I love to be able to do that when I am eighty!). Maintaining an orchard is a hobby of theirs, and they opened their home to share with me. During our first meeting, Toby would occasionally get up, pull a loaf of sheepherder's bread out of the oven, and check it. Finally, it was ready. We were still talking. She cut open the warm bread, slathered a layer of butter on it, and with wide, expressive, caring eyes, offered it to me. What was I to do? I thanked her graciously and ate it.

True, I felt more fatigued from eating this bread later. I think I am more aware of the effects of processed foods now. But it wasn't a big deal. When he was sending his disciples out, Jesus also said, "And if you drink any deadly thing, it shall not hurt you." That inspires me in the bigger picture. Ultimately, we regenerate. It is done, gone from my body, and her warm smile lingers.

However, for me it is different when the children are involved. I think many of our traditions have evolved into junk-food fests and it is time to revisit them and think more creatively. For example, a local mom, who is originally from China, recently brought in a cake to celebrate the New Moon, which is a traditional Chinese celebration. She was kind enough to bring in literature on the tradition. Interestingly, the "cake" traditionally was ground lotus seed formed into cakes (and perhaps dehydrated by the sun?). From what I can gather, it has now evolved into refined sugar and flour fest. I wonder how else our traditions have evolved (or degenerated).

Every situation is different, and I try to let intuition guide me. I know there are times when I could have done better.

Let Jeff tell you about our Halloween:

> Halloween can be challenging for the obvious reasons: candy, candy, and more candy. Being our first "Raw Halloween," we wanted to make it a special, fun night so the children didn't feel like they were missing out. So we turned our house into a haunted house.
>
> I went to the local store and bought the necessary props (black lights, flying bats, rats, witches, etc.). June made "blood" beverages: pomegranate juice for the kids and a lime-, apple-, ginger-, beet-juice combo for the adults. We added dry ice to this, which made a great witch's brew. We all dressed up, put on June's "Eternal Om" background music, and had a blast. Our kids even invited some of their friends to help work in the haunted house. We handed out glow necklaces instead of candy. (June: "We are on the lookout for more inexpensive, environmentally friendly gifts or little toys for next year. Stick-on tattoos might be good.")
>
> The kids really liked to get something besides candy. Plus, the glow necklaces were a safety bonus because cars could see them at night. We had kids and parents coming back to the house two and three times. June was handing out the smoking drinks. Our house was a great community pit stop. All in all, it was a huge success. It was a fair amount of work, but the kids had a wonderful time. We may make it a tradition; we will see.
>
> One of our ten-year-old daughters did want to take a break from the haunted house and go trick-or-treating with her friend. When they were done, she gave all her candy to her friends back at the house by dipping her "empty" hand in the dry ice and coming out with her candy. They all enjoyed it.

Question: Regarding protein: before starting this for my whole family, I would want lots of info that their daily nutrition needs could be adequately met (Chris, Pacific Palisades).

Response: I would recommend going to the library and checking out some of the books in the index, especially *The China Study*. There are some great reads on how we digest amino acids more directly from plant food and the strong level of proteins in leaves, sprouts, sprouted seeds, seaweeds, and super foods. I have doctors that agree with me and others that are more cautious; it's new territory for them (and generally speaking, medical doctors have only a few required hours of nutrition in their curriculum). Even the doctor who gave me the blood test was skeptical, and before the results came back, he expressed doubt in my diet and suggested eating meat. However, when the tests came back, he was very confident in my diet and firmly supports me in continuing on this path. He also pressed me to tell him what supplements I was taking. "No supplements," I said, "just whole foods."

A 30 percent protein diet is achievable with leaves, sprouts, seeds, fruits, veggies, and some super foods (spirulina, blue-green algae, bee pollen, which have a higher level of protein than animal proteins).

However, our pediatrician isn't at all concerned about our children's protein levels. In his forty years of thriving practice, he has never seen protein deficiency. With him, we discuss how the diet of our culture seems way off track. In terms of our SAD (Standard American Diet), we are strongly influenced, even (white) lied to, from marketing and advertising (from junk food to pharmaceutical to diet pills), lobbying (take a look at the dairy, meat, and grain representation on the food pyramid—and where are the leaves?), and subsidizing (a steak costs only a fraction of the price it would if the government didn't subsidize), so our diet has gone askew.

Chris, I know you also have a Judeo-Christian background, so this also might be of interest to you. Check it out, Genesis 1:29: "And God said, 'See, I have given you every herb that yields seed which is on the face of all the earth, and every tree whose fruit yields seed: to you it shall be for food.'" That is it!

(Now, if you take the story of Noah literally, when he got off the ark, he looked around and there weren't a lot of seeds, herbs, or fruits in sight. So he talked with God and at that point God gave Noah the temporary go ahead to eat "every moving thing that lives … but not flesh with its life or blood." (Gen 9:3-4) Then in Leviticus (3:17) God makes a final statement about it: "This shall be a perpetual statute throughout your generations in all your dwellings: you shall eat neither fat nor blood.")

But getting back to Genesis 1:29: I find it fascinating. Especially in light of the article I just read in the paper, "Humans' Beef with Livestock: A Warmer Planet." The news is out. "American Meat Eaters are responsible for one and a half more tons of C02 (per person, annually) than vegetarians." (*Christian Science Monitor*, Feb 20, 2007, referencing research from the University of Chicago).

But the real whopper is the latest information on how methane contributes twenty-three times more to global warming than CO2. Livestock is the largest contributor of anthropogenic methane (37 percent!) and growing. However, "methane cycles out of the atmosphere in just eight years" (Earth Save Report: "A New Global Warming Strategy: How Environmentalists Are Overlooking Vegetarianism as the Most Effective Tool Against Climate Change in Our Lifetimes by Noam Mohr," earthsave.org). So we have at our fingertips a quick, simple (no, not easy) *solution to immediately reverse the global warming trend*.

On the flip side, the above-mentioned article points out that as prosperity increases, so does our meat consumption. That, "between 1970 and 2002, annual per capita meat consumption in developing countries rose from 24 pounds to 64 pounds, according to the Food and Agriculture Organization of the United Nations (FAO)." Between 1970 and 2002, as populations increased, total meat consumption in the developing world grew nearly fivefold.

The article goes on to say, "annual global meat production is projected to more than double from 229 million tons at the beginning of the decade to 465 million tons in 2050. That makes livestock the fastest growing sector of global agriculture."

This seems a sad misinterpretation of this counsel: "Take no thought for your life, what ye shall eat or what ye shall drink" (Mathew 6:31). Don't think about these things?

No—I understand this quote to mean "take no anxious thought." Do not worry about if there will be food on the table, trust and follow divine Love, and Love will provide for all our needs.

I, too, wonder about how to let go of anxious thinking. Even though the stats might look depressing, let's look at it this way. The average American today eats 134 hamburgers a year. However, the first fast-food hamburger joint opened up in the 1920s. If we look at how quickly (less than a century) we have climbed to 134 hamburgers per person, it could take less than a century to make a 180 degree turn.

Ultimately, we take a perceived risk in this culture if we stop eating meat, but our children have so much more to gain, as a global family, from taking that risk. And the food—you can learn to *love* it.

Question: Is there a spectrum of "rawness"? In other words, is it better to not even use the dehydrator? (Mihaela, Ojai, CA)

Response: Here's my spectrum: First of all, at the top, is whole, *living* foods: Sprouts, germinated seeds, anything that you could put in the garden and it would grow. (I haven't planted my buckwheat crackers, but some whole germinated buckwheat survived the food processor, and I think a cracker might even grow buckwheat if planted). Secondly, would be whole, *raw* food: fresh leaves, fruit off the vine, germinated nuts. Thirdly, more prepared raw food that makes the transition to raw food delightful and delicious. From there I would rank the following:

4. Frozen whole food
5. Dehydrated food
6. Cooked food
7. Cooked leftovers, microwaved food, and processed foods

We are all on our own paths, doing the best we can, and some days we have better options than others, and *it is okay. Just do the best you can.*

Question: After hearing about some of the places where you compromised (like on dairy for the kids or on maple syrup), it seemed realistic on the one hand, but made me wish you didn't do it on the other. For me, it's easier to follow a big changeover if the rules are in stone—not open at all. (Chris, Pacific Palisades, Ca)

Response: For me, the black and white approach worked better, too, because I wanted to really give this a try and move out of the migraine phase of my life. In fact, I think it was key in my healing (*all* whole, raw food and natural cosmetic and cleaning products). However, for my family, given the culture we are living in, it was too drastic for them. Think in terms of progress in our food choices—not in terms of perfection—or it is too overwhelming. This way, the family becomes a healthy circle in which to support each other.

Every family sets their own standards. On our raw journey, we met parents who shared with us that they felt it was really important not to pasteurize. We started purchasing only raw dairy from highly reputable, quality dairies. Moving away from pasteurized dairy was a good first step for us. But now, except for raw goat cheese and occasionally butter, the kids are off dairy. They haven't asked for cream the past couple months, so I'm not buying it.

I think blanching my veggies every once in a while (steaming veggies for a minute and then submerging them in cold water, see "Super Simple Soup") is not going to do any harm. It doesn't offer as many nutrients as raw veggies, but it offers a happy medium when extended family and friends are over for a meal.

I also wonder if I had made my family go cold turkey with me, if it could have been detrimental—especially if someone is going from a low-fiber diet to a high-fiber diet overnight. They might have some major plumbing problems.

It is important to transition to raw food gradually. For me, it was eliminating processed food for two months and then going for it. For the children, it has been more gradual, and we are not done. Asking the children to go from pizza, French fries, chicken nuggets, fruit juice, corn, and cookies to a 100 percent raw diet overnight would be too much—for anyone! Sometimes the progress is fast, sometimes slow—one step forward, two steps back—but stepping back and looking at the overall progress, it is exciting. I hope this book opens up possibilities to that complete transition.

One key in the transition was the green smoothies (see "Super Green Power Smoothie" recipe). I think by just starting with that in the morning and moving away from the white carbohydrates, the door will start to open. I suggest doing that for a month or two and then start learning about the raw diet more, reading raw books and searching Google for "raw recipes." Then, do a few days a week totally raw and finally, yet gradually, make the break.

Question: Can you suggest some meals: a breakfast, snack, lunch, snack, dinner, dessert? (Deborah, Malibu, CA)

Response: Yes, but before I do, remember to also get some sunshine daily, exercise, spend some time being prayerful or meditating, and read from an inspiring "raw" book. The books are important because they open a whole new way of thinking. I know I needed to deprogram from the media and my schooling and open up my thought.

Breakfast: "Super Power Smoothie," a large glass or two if you are hungry. If you're still hungry, have the "Berry Crunch" or "Rah Rah Cereal" with "Hemp Mylk" and blueberries, but I think you will fill up on the smoothie. The point is, don't limit your quantities. Eat as much as your body wants. I think it is really hard to overeat raw food.

Snack: If you get hungry before lunch, have fruit (perhaps a coconut), or the bowl of cereal. Charlotte likes to have the "High Flying Apple Sandwiches." I like "Strawberry Crackers" with hemp butter, covered with sliced nectarines or blueberries and topped with sprouted quinoa.

Lunch: "Buckwheat Raw Crackers" with avocado and a big bunch of sprouts sprinkled on top, with a pinch of Herbamere. Or a low fat, simpler option is a large plate of seasonal fruit.

Snack: Crudités (red peppers, cucumber, celery, etc.) and if you are really hungry, dip the crudités in the "Avocado (not so skinny) Dip." A glass of the "Lemonaid" with chia seeds might be nice now, or just before dinner.

Dinner: A large salad of your heart's desire (see some of the salad recipes) with the "Caesar Salad Dressing." I might sprinkle sunflower seeds on it.

Dessert: If you are not done yet, I'm surprised. But you might have a late night snack of another large plate of veggies or a "Chocolate Chip Cookie" or blend up some "Hot Chocolate" with mesquite and maca powder.

With all the recipes I just mentioned, I would forgo maple sugar, honey, and banana (I haven't given up dates yet—see the back of this book for a list of foods to avoid or limit) just so you can experience raw and clean out the sugar addiction. It makes the diet much more enjoyable.

If you don't want to spend much time in the kitchen, stock the kitchen with seasonal fruits, cucumbers, celery, and bell peppers. You can buy the raw cereal, hemp milk, crackers, and butters. I like to make these because I like it really fresh, and, for a family of six, buying it ready made at the store can get expensive (and use excessive packaging). I used to get "Karma" or "Lydia's" cereal and crackers in the raw section of our local Co-op.

This time when you settle into bed in the evening, spend some time just enjoying the quiet. Notice how good you feel and perhaps have a gratitude moment.

Question: Do you have a weekly meal plan for the family? (Sydney, Malibu, CA)

Response: We sat down as a family and came up with lists. This is one of the lists that the girls have chosen that Jeff and I support—win/win choices.

Breakfast Requests:
   "Super Green Power Smoothie" (we do this most mornings)
   Seasonal Fruit
   "Berry Crunch Cereal" (the kids mix in Ezekiel 4:9 Sprouted Grain Cereal by Food for Life, Barbara's Shredded Spoonfuls or Shredded Oats) with Almond or Hempseed Mylk and berries
   "Yummy French Toast" with sliced bananas and strawberries

Children's Sandwich Requests:
   Seasonal Fruit and "Rah! Rah! Cereal Bars"
   Whole-wheat pita and hummus with avocado and lettuce
   Sprouted bread with "Vegan Tuna," avocado, and lettuce
   "Fly High Apple Pie Sandwiches"
   Toasted sprouted bread with almond butter and sliced bananas, berries, raw honey or unsweetened jam
   Pigs in a Blanket (celery with almond butter)

Note: with these lunches, they always have a fruit, dried fruit, (raw) cookies or carob balls, and sometimes celery or cucumber. If we don't have raw cookies, they like "Fabe's" whole grain, all natural cookies (but they are cooked).

Dinner Requests:
    "Spring Rolls"
    "Sushi"
    Avocado on "Rah! Rah! Crackers" with Salad
    "Super Simple Soup and Salad"
    "Tomato Soup" and "Kid's Salad" with sprouted toast
    "Vegan Tuna" and "Kid's Salad" and sprouted toast
    Quinoa and salad with artichoke (steamed or raw, see "Raw Artichoke")
    All the favorites recipes you'll find under "What We Think: A Kid's Perspective"

Note: The salad always has hemp seeds and/or sprouted quinoa and sesame seeds for protein (including the EFA Omega-3).

Dessert Requests
    (raw) "Chocolate Chip Cookies"
    "Carob Balls"
    (raw) "Peach Pie with Vanilla Ice Cream"
    Banana Splits (see "Fly High Apple Pie Sandwich" recipe)
    "Coconut Brownie Macaroons"
    "Chocolate—Raw!"
    Cut orange and apple
    Tangerines
    Grapes

Question: When vegetables are briefly cooked in minimal water so that none is tossed out, are enough nutrients retained to justify their use? (Mary, Carmel, CA)

Response: Yes, in moderation. Ideally, at least 80 percent of our food is raw (unaltered and unprocessed). However, some vegetables, including potatoes, are better for digestion when cooked. (If you eat them, legumes, including beans, peanuts, fava beans, kidney beans, black beans, and soybeans are also best cooked).

Steaming or blanching vegetables (setting them in hot water, often for a soup) can be a nice treat in the winter (see "Super Simple Soup").

Last night we had steamed artichoke for an appetizer and the children went wild repeating, "I love artichoke!" When the soup arrived from our local vegan restaurant, Charlotte, age four, exclaimed, "I love spinach soup!" If that is going to be a source of vegetables for the children, wonderful!

However, the nature of the vegetables changes when even briefly cooked. They become more glycemic, and we lose up to 50 percent of our protein when we cook our vegetables.

Personally, as I am healing, I find living and raw foods to be much more "vital," full of life, and more satiating.

Question: Sometimes when I serve a raw meal, the kids fall apart, complaining and whining. It would be so much easier to call out for a pizza or feed them a hamburger with French fries and soda. Any suggestions?

Response: I have been there, and it's no fun! Children will test you to see how far you will go. It must be their job. My job is to feed them good food.

Try to remain calm but firm. If the younger ones throw a tantrum, they need to leave the room for a few minutes to pull themselves together (and sometimes it is me who needs the time out). Once they know the boundaries, they will stop whining and testing us, and we can settle down and have a wonderful, memorable meal together as a family.

Remember to get the children involved in meal preparation, from start to finish. If you don't have a kitchen garden for them to connect with the food, make sure they go to the farmer's market with you to select the food for the week. Encourage them to touch and smell these new foods as they help you prepare them. They might even start coming up with favorite recipes of their own. Invite them to select the recipes from this book and help you plan the special meals for that week. Or you can let each member of the family plan and help prepare one balanced dinner each week. (Then, when they move out, they'll have successful survival skills in place.)

I heard recently that many children will not accept a new food until it has been offered at least ten times. (American Academy of Pediatrics, *Pediatric Nutrition Handbook, Fourth Edition*, Elk Grove Village, IL, 1998). So don't give up. With new food, I only ask that they try two bites (and their rule with me is that they will try the two bites only if I really think they might like it—fortunately they still trust me). After a few of these two-bite sessions, I often find one of the children starts requesting the food. Soon, hopefully, the whole gang jumps on board. However, until they do, I try not to serve the food as part of the main course. Instead, the new food is served as an appetizer until it is accepted into the family fare.

Chapter Eleven:
Organic, Local, and Seasonal

Have you ever groaned when the ice cream truck comes along, spewing out fumes from the truck, carrying heavily processed and chemically loaded ice creams in plastic wrappers that are made halfway across the country? (Not to mention the music that calls the kids like cows to the dinner bell?)

When we buy locally we have more knowledge about our purchases, food tastes better, and the global impact of transporting the goods is gone. We have less risk of, say, finding rat poising in our cat food or lead paint in our children's toys; we can learn what metals our processed foods have come in contact with and what level of organic we are supporting (a large commercial USDA organic farm or a trusted relationship with a small farm that takes organic to a whole new level by using a system of composting, crop rotation, energy and water conservation, etc.).

Also, eating seasonally rather than importing our fruit from New Zealand and not overdoing a fruit or vegetable makes sense, doesn't it? Our bodies were meant to intake a variety of foods, and the seasons ensure this. In the summer, we eat more fresh fruit, and we eat more dried fruit in the winter (including "Fruit Leathers"—the kids love these in their lunches.)

Finally, there is considerable debate over eating local versus organic. We can pay considerably more for organic apples shipped across the country. Or should we choose the fresher, less expensive, conventional, local varieties? As far as raw is concerned, the fresher the better, but nothing justifies putting toxins in our environment (or our bodies). The toll of these toxins pouring into our waterways and shorelines, on our farmers and field workers (showing higher rates of cancer), on our food chain and nutrient supply, not to mention the CO_2 released and the global warming factor—it is daunting. Then there is the CO_2 spent in making the fertilizers, herbicides, and pesticides and delivering them to the crop; the cost of conventional produce is too great.

The USDA has its flaws. We have wondered, considering the loosening regulations on organic: is organic really organic? Here is an interesting Web site: http://www. restoreorganiclaw.org. It helped me understand why some people laugh when I share my enthusiasm for organic fruits and vegetables: they are on a different page, eating organic, *processed* food. (Sounds like an oxymoron, doesn't it?) It looks to me like it is the organic, *processed* food that might not be so organic because companies, especially the large-scale industrial-agro businesses, add in synthetic additives. Also, prewashed salad greens can be washed with chlorinated water (washed with ... chlorine?), and can still be called "organic" by the USDA, and not have to inform the consumer. The discussion brings along with it inspiration for everyone with even a sunny window sill (think sprouts), to have their own kitchen garden. Still, when we buy organic *produce*, excluding chlorine-washed greens and sprouts, odds still look good that organic is really organic.

Even though the product might have the USDA label, look for more honorable/ alternative-certification organizations as well, such as Oregon Tilth, California Certified Organic Farmers, Marin Organic Certifying Agency, and Demeter Certified Biodynamic.

With the raw diet, tracing the food source as well as eating local and organic becomes much easier. (And more affordable! The price of corn and gas is driving up food prices, except for locally grown, raw food.) The bulk of the food our family consumes is local produce. Here in Los Angeles, local produce (fruits and vegetables, fresh herbs and leaves) is abundant, with farmer's markets and food co-ops available. I have developed a homing device of sorts for "USDA-certified organic" signs. If I can't find the produce I'm looking for, I'll occasionally settle for the "pesticides-free" signs, but only after grilling the farmer on his choice of fertilizer. John, one of the farmers at our local farmers market, sells big bunches of nettles, lamb's quarters, and purslane for one dollar each! (And doesn't charge for carrot and radish tops.) Think of it: the most important food is the cheapest and easiest to grow.

If we don't make it to our local farmer's market, Organic Express (see "Where to Find It") will affordably deliver to the door fresh, seasonal produce.

With the help of greenhouses, berries, avocados, and many of our favorites grow year round. (If you live in a colder climate, forgive me: I just want to remind myself and the other locals here that this is achievable.) However, be careful not to overdo a food. Too much of a good thing can turn bad. Our bodies need a variety of foods, and the four seasons bring this variety.

The remainder of our food is what makes raw cuisine more interesting: dried fruit, nuts (minimized) and seeds, spelt, buckwheat, and some grains and beans (cooked). Some of these items come from our local farmer's market: almonds, pecans, walnuts, macadamia nuts, honey and bee pollen, olives and olive oil, dates, dried fruit—and they taste so much better when they are fresh and local. Some organic staples are not available locally. I order them by mail. Sun Organic Farm supplies most of our needs.

The following is a list of our staples from Sun Organic Farm that are not local: Maple syrup from Maine; buckwheat and spelt from the drier plains of the Midwest; hemp seeds from Canada; sesame, flax, and chia seeds; quinoa, cacao, cinnamon, and vanilla from Central and South America; and coconut oil and dried coconut (no sulfites and raw) from the Philippines. Spices come from India and the Indian Peninsula. However, back to local versus Organic: my organic sunflower and pumpkin seeds come from China. However, these items could be grown and purchased locally if there was a stronger, local, *raw, and organic* market. (Vote!)

My other dried-food supplier, Sunfood Nutrition (sunfood.com) is committed to supporting the indigenous farmer, often paying 25 percent more to support the local infrastructure (look for the Sunfood Nutrition label). My Sunfood Nutrition products are raw cashews (another food I want to move away from, but it gives a creamy smooth consistency to our desserts) from Indonesia; cacao (butter, beans, powder, and nibs) from Ecuador; vanilla beans from Papua New Guinea; Nori sheets; other seaweeds and pistachios from Asia; (raw) agave light and dark nectar from Mexico; yacon syrup and mesquite powder from Peru. Whew!

So, yes, not everything is local. I'd say approximately 80 percent of our food budget is seasonal and locally grown. Perhaps our next step in this adventure will be eating just what is raw and local. Instead of being "locavores," we can push it to the next level, "frugi-loco-vores."

When our family purchases imported goods, I'm now, finally, making a point to check for humane-labor practices. For example, do you know where your sugar is coming from? What about the sugar that is in America's favorite candy bars? I was recently reading about cane cutters in Nicaragua and El Salvador who work long hours and make one dollar and eighty cents *a day*, only to face kidney failure (could it be the chemical pesticides? Two thousand people are recorded with this illness, five hundred and sixty dead and counting, *The Miami Herald, Cancun Edition,* May 6, 2007) after two or more years of field work. These workers are often unable to live off the land (owned by the plantation owners) and essentially live like paid slaves—and 80 percent of this sugar is being shipped to the United States! Oh, the social cost of sugar.

On the flip side, purchasing organic, fair-trade cacao beans from Ecuador (or Brazil) supports the rainforests! Here's an example of a "global vote." Cacao trees rely on the canopy of the rainforests for protection from the sun. So, here we have a direct opportunity to support our planet's rainforests.

I figure a purchase that supports more trees on this planet is worthwhile, including nuts, maple syrup, mesquite (which is becoming endangered in some areas; it is being plundered for furniture), coconuts, vanilla, olives, bananas, and dates. If these foods support fair trade and strengthen indigenous communities, purchasing them sends a strong message. It is a worthwhile vote.

The best place to find local, organic, and seasonal produce is in our own backyards. In the Loukses' backyard, we have three raised beds. Our backyard is also an experiment (another adventure) in goji berries (previously from the Himalayan Mountains), aloe (from Mexico), stevia, fruit trees, a few herbs (lemon grass for the Thai Soup), weeds, and a host of other berries (the children love it). It's a journey.

Chapter Twelve: Where to Find It

Organic Produce:

Your backyard!

Farmers Markets

The Local Co-opportunity or a Co-operative Farm

Organic Express (go to www.spud.com—California only, San Francisco: 415-ORGANIC, LA: 310-ORGANIC) Organic Express delivers fresh produce to your door.

Trader Joe's (we have found organic almonds at Trader Joe's for a good price), Whole Foods, Wild Oats

Your local grocery store (put on your organic homing device, head for the back corner of the produce section, and be prepared to pay a pretty penny)

Freshly Pressed Oils:

Andreas Seed Oil Company, Oak Park, CA, 805-443-2300 Andreas.wecker@gmail.com (Andreas supplies us weekly with freshly pressed flaxseed oil)

Dried Staples:

Sun Organic Farm (sunorganic.com, 888-269-9888, I'm impressed with the consistent freshness of their staples) Note: Refrigerate any nuts, seeds, or dried fruits you are not using. Nuts, especially, because of their fat content, can go rancid fairly quickly.

Tree of Life (treeoflife.com, 520-394-2520); also has books and videos by Dr. Gabriel Cousens

Sunfood Nutrition (sunfood.com, 888-RAW-FOOD, also sells raw books and CDs, kitchen appliances, nut mylk bags, glass straws, mesquite powder, and super foods)

It's important not to store your staples (grains, nuts, seeds, dried foods) on your shelves. Keep it moving so it's always fresh. If you won't be using it soon, refrigerate or freeze it. Flaxseeds and nuts have the shortest shelf life. If they lose their crunch or yellow, they may be rancid.

Appliances:

Tribest Corporation (tribestlife.com, 888-254-7336); sproutman.com; sunfood.com; and if you are in the Santa Monica area, go to Don Kidson's Busy Bee Hardware Store because Don has the Teflex sheets for the dehydrator available for order.

Plastic Bag/Cup Alternatives:

Reusablebags.com (888-707-3873—great reusable alternative for kids' lunches, water bottles, etc.): This Web site is a great resource of information. For example, did you know that we are "globally consuming over 1 million plastic bags per minute?" And "these plastic bags don't biodegrade, they photo degrade—breaking down into smaller and smaller toxic bits contaminating soil and waterways and entering the food web when animals accidentally ingest." Also, "hundreds of thousands of sea turtles, whales, and other marine animals die every year from eating discarded plastic bags mistaken for food." Finally, there is hope, "In 2001, Ireland consumed 1.2 billion plastic bags, or 316 per person. An extremely successful plastic bag consumption tax … introduced in 2002, reduced consumption by 90 percent. Approximately 18,000,000 liters of oil have been saved due to this reduced production."

Trellisearth.com (760-494-2000- biodegradable corn based cups): Think of how many plastic cups go in the trash and landfills. I met with the food and beverage director of our local beach club about switching to biodegradable cups and they are going with it! Do you have any clubs in your area that might cant to know about this alternative?

Wet Products, Inc: Biodegradable water balloons.

Other:

Co-op America (coopamerica.org): National-membership opportunity and resource guide for companies that put people and the planet first; find out which companies are degrading our environment and treating communities irresponsibly.

Catalogchoice.com makes it easy to unsubscribe to the catalogs that arrive in the mail. Save our trees.

Chapter Thirteen:
Loukses' List of Foods to Avoid and Minimize

For long-term health

Many of these foods are staples of the American Diet we are still gently moving away from as a family. Remember, it's about progress, not perfection. The recipes in this book have not avoided all the foods on this list but have eliminated most and reduced the remaining few to small amounts.

Genetically Modified Foods (GMOs): wheat, soy (including soy milk), potatoes, corn. These are also hybridized foods you might want to move away from, along with refined sugar.

Incidentally, the above-mentioned foods are on the list of foods people are most highly allergic to (as well as dairy, shellfish, tomatoes, and peanuts, see *Depression Free Living* by Dr. Gabriel Cousens). This association makes me wonder: we might not want to alter (genetically modify, or even hybridize) what our ecosystem and we as a species have evolved on. These foods have been modified to alter taste, adapt to large-scale, industrial agriculture, increase shelf life, and/or decrease susceptibility to insects or disease. All of these modifications help to increase bottom-line profits, but do they support health?

Processed Foods: Wheat or "enriched" flour (also known as white flour), white rice, white pasta, refined sugar, brown sugar, powdered sugar, molasses, corn derivatives

Fungi: Mushrooms, peanuts, and if you can, cashews. (Peanuts have an especially high array of toxins, notably aflatoxin, which researchers have shown to cause liver cancer.)

Chemicals: Preservatives (sulfates, sulfites—usually in dried fruit, xanthan gum), artificial sweeteners, conventional produce (especially for children)

Animal Products: see introduction, *The China Study*

High Glycemic Foods: Refined sugar, high fructose corn syrup, pasteurized fruit juice

Cooked Oils (except coconut oil, as coconut oil is stable even under high heat; extra-virgin olive oil on low to medium heat is fine)

Drugs and Alcohol: Alcohol is the most acidic food. Drugs, even caffeine, also tend to make us more acidic.

Mycotoxins: Mycotoxins include all of the above-listed foods, beans, yeasts, stored grains, cashews, and *more* (believe it our not), according to Dr. Cousens (see *Rainbow Green Live Food Cuisine*)

Note: Soy crops are cutting into the rainforests. If you eat animal or soy products, find out where the soy is grown. The European community has recently discovered that although they stopped purchasing beef raised on the deforested land of original rainforests, they were purchasing livestock that was fed soy grown on these lands: "Nearly 80 percent of the soy harvested around the world ends up as animal feed. Only about 6 percent of the global soy crop is harvested for direct human consumption in products such as soy milk and tofu," *Nature Conservancy Magazine*, Autumn, 2007.

Foods to Minimize
For a lean, clean, thriving machine!

Salt: Salt in an inorganic form can be a poison. However, sodium, in an organic form (found in celery and tomatoes), is healthful; it is an essential mineral. When you are ready, substitute salt for celery in the crackers, dressings, and soups in the recipes found in this book.

Sweeteners: Refined stevia; maple granules; date granules; agave nectar; honey (babies should not be fed honey until they are two years old); fresh-squeezed juice.

Produce: Heavily hybridized foods, including carrots and seedless fruits. Root vegetables and legumes because when they are raw, they are often difficult to digest (except maca powder).

Oils: Oils are fats without the fiber (and therefore should be minimized). Stone-pressed oils are best and then cold-pressed oils. Also, nutrient-rich oils like hemp or flaxseed oils are best, so consider substituting these oils for olive oil in salad dressings. Avoid products that use a heat process to extract the oil. Extra-virgin oil is the least processed. Better whole-food options (fats with their fiber intact), are avocado, soaked chia seeds, ground flaxseeds in smoothies, whole olives soaked in water, and coconuts eaten as a meal.

Nuts: Go easy on the nuts. Nuts are dessert—high in fat. The following nuts should be soaked in water to release the enzyme inhibitors, toxins, and make them more digestible:
    Almonds: twelve hours; Walnuts and Pecans: one hour

Soy Condiments: Namu Shoyu and Miso, especially the lighter-colored, more-processed varieties.

If you or your family members are prone to kidney stones, minimize:

Greens High in Oxalic Acid: Spinach, chard, beet tops, amaranth greens, parsley, endive, escarole, watercress, chives, scallions, mature mustard greens

Chapter Fourteen:
"Emergency" Foods
We Keep in the Car

Whenever I go to pick up the girls from school, I bring snacks with me that won't easily make a mess in the car. Cucumbers, celery, apples, cut oranges, bananas, watermelon, melon, peaches, and apricots work great. Berries, cherries, and pomegranates are off the list.

There are other great raw foods that also keep the messes under control:

Dried fruits and fruit leathers

Nuts and seeds (especially a small bag of chia seeds—see "Lemon Chia Seed Drink")

Lara Bars or Vega Whole Food Energy Bars (myvega.com, 800-839-8863)

"Berry Crunch Cereal" or "Rah! Rah! Cereal Bars"

Left-over plastic produce bags and *napkins* are always great to have on hand for easy cleanup.

Chapter Fifteen:
Twenty-one-day Meal Plan

Made easy and simple

It takes twenty-one days to create a new habit. Before you start your twenty-one days, take a few days to prepare (or buy online from your favorite raw-foods store) the following: fresh, organic, local produce. This is the most important, and if you are not able to do anything else, this is your key ingredient. To help ease the transition, you also might want to have the following on hand: "Berry Crunch Cereal" (or the available raw cereal from the store), "Almond or Hemp Mylk," "Buckwheat (or otherwise raw) Crackers," "Strawberry Crackers," "Caesar Salad Dressing" (or a purchased, raw, salad dressing, try Organicville Sesame Tamari Vinaigrette), "Fermented Coconut," "Fermented Veggies" (available with Healing Movement), "Heirloom Tomato Variantes" (I haven't seen this in stores) and "Chocolate Chip Cookies" (if you can find a raw cookie you like in the stores that does the job, go for it). Keep hemp seed on hand to make more "Hemp Mylk" as needed.

For all the breakfasts in this twenty-one-day plan, use variations of the "Super Green Power Smoothie," being careful to start slowly with the amount of greens and super foods, building as you go, so that is tastes delicious to you. If you need more for breakfast or need a mid-morning snack, I suggest several of the same fruit (for better digestion, versus lots of different fruits), cucumbers, or one of the cereals with sprouts and "Hemp Mylk."

For all the dinners, I suggest soup and/or a large salad of your choice from the dinner section of this book. You can vary your salad toppings with a variety of seeds. (Idea: if salads get boring, remember it is all in the leaves, and there you should have a variety of leaves. If you have a good window sill, or small vegetable bed, plant an assortment of leaves. The children enjoy harvesting dinner, and the fresh variety is mouthwatering.) If you still have room after dinner and would like a dessert, make your selection from the afternoon delights or dessert section of this book. Take care to wait a few hours before eating fruit after a large dinner. Also, refrain from eating for two hours before going to bed, until breaking the fast in the morning.

Be sure to drink plenty of water, exercise, and relax a few minutes each day in the sunshine. Educate yourself by reading from raw mentors. Start a journal and daily note your favorite foods, any obstacles, and the progress you are noticing. Most importantly, if you don't already do so, begin the practice of meditating for a half hour each day, starting with five minutes and building from there.

For meditation, find a quiet spot. If there is no quiet spot, I will light candles, hold hands, and have the family join me. Sometimes, I begin with emptying my mind of activity through deep-breathing exercises, mentally drinking in life, love, and what is true, as well as exhaling (letting go of) what is no longer useful. With the family, we always begin and end with three "Oms." Usually, I'll begin by meditating on inspired scripture. Meditations can focus on gratitude or compassion. Sometimes I like to focus on my favorite affirmations:

"I forgive easily and maintain my state of wellbeing throughout the day."
"My moderate, principled living is attracted to, embraces, and receives Love."
"I live in harmony with the natural laws of the universe."
"Fulfillment and satisfaction come from my balanced, principled living and free expression."
"I express abundant energy, deeper patience, creativity, and natural, vibrant beauty."
"I am radiantly healthy."
"I am an attractor field for ideas, solutions, synergy, and connection."

This deepening spiritual awareness will then better guide my food choices.

Keep the portions moderate. Less food is always better than too much, and easier on digestion. Be mindful not to make your portions too small, leaving you feeling hungry. If an upcoming meal looks too complicated, or you don't have the ingredients available, repeat a meal on the 21-day plan that has worked easily for you (especially if it will help simplify your preparations). *Feed yourself with plenty of food*, minimizing nuts and processed oils, and instead eating more seeds, avocados and coconuts when you feel you need more fat. *Let your growing intuition and growing ability to listen to your body be your guides.*

If letting go of refined sugar or white flour is difficult, try to have a fermented food every day. I found it was especially helpful in overcoming sugar addictions. A spoonful of "Fermented Veggies" with lunch or evening salad or "Fermented Coconut" with your breakfast cereal might be a good place to start.

Lunch can be as simple as a large helping of fresh fruit. Alternatively, you might want transition food. So let's get started with some lunch ideas:

Day One:
    Breakfast: "Super Green Power Smoothie" (page 3, typical)
    Lunch: Two heaping scoops of "Fermented Coconut," topped with fresh seasonal fruit and "Berry Crunch Cereal."
    Afternoon snack: Crudités with "Avocado (not so skinny) Dip" and/or "Lemon Chia Seed Drink"
    Dinner: Soup and/or Salad of your choice (see pages 35-53 typical)
    (If it is easier for your schedule, you can switch the lunch for dinner and vice versa and even switch the days around, depending on what you have in the refrigerator.)

Day Two:
    Lunch: "Vegan Tuna Sandwich" with "Fermented Veggies"
    Afternoon snack: "Coconut Fizz"

Day 3:
    Lunch: "Fly High Apple Pie Sandwich"
    Afternoon snack: "Easy Banana Ice Cream" or "Lemon Chia Seed Drink"

Day 4:
    Lunch: "Avocado and Crackers" topped with sprouts and "Fermented Veggies" on the side
    Afternoon snack: Popsicle (see popsicle recipes)

Day 5:
    Lunch: "Heather's Scrumptious Purple Cabbage Delight"
    Afternoon snack: "Watermelon Delight"

Day 6:
    Lunch: Saladacco zucchini on a bed of greens
    Afternoon snack: "Sapote with Lime"

Day 7:
    Lunch: "Spring Rolls"
    Afternoon snack: "Melon Delight"

Day 8:
    Lunch: "Avocado and Crackers" with a side of Tabouli
    Afternoon snack: "Chocolate Mylk"

Day 9:
    Lunch: "Strawberry Crackers" with hemp butter and sliced fruit, sprinkled with sprouted quinoa (see "Tabouli" recipe)
    Afternoon snack: "Pumpkin Seed Crunchies" and "Lemonaid"

Day 10:
    Lunch: "Banana Boats"
    Afternoon snack: "Nanette's Hummus" (optional) with crudités

Day 11:
    Lunch: "Summer Sushi"
    Afternoon Snack: "Cinnamon Apples"

Day 12:
    Lunch: "Olga's Heirloom Tomatoes"
    Afternoon Snack: "Gingeraid"

Day 13:
    Lunch: "Thai Pizza"
    Afternoon snack: Fresh Fruit

Day 14:
    Lunch: "Primo Pesto Pasta"
    Afternoon Snack: Strawberries and Cream

Day 15:
    Lunch: Crackers, topped "Garlic Lover's Cream Cheeze," grated beets, and pea sprouts
    Afternoon Snack: One Whole Cucumber

Day 16:
    Lunch: "Primo Pesto Pizza"
    Afternoon snack: Cabbage Crunchies (cabbage broken into pieces the size of potato chips)

Day 17:
    Lunch: "Fly High Apple Pie Sandwiches"
    Afternoon Snack: "Easy Cheesecake" or Fresh Fruit

Day 18:
    Lunch: "Cucumber/Tahini Spelt Bread Sandwich" (substitute with crackers on hand if necessary)
    Afternoon Snack: "Hot Chocolate"

Day 19:
    Lunch: Cheeze and Crackers, topped with radish or broccoli sprouts
    Afternoon Snack: Coconut water and flesh

Day 20:
    Lunch: Bowl of "Tabouli"
    Afternoon Snack: Watermelon

Day 21:
    Lunch: "Power Raspberries"
    Afternoon snack: Celery and Cauliflower florets with optional "Avocado (not so skinny) Dip"

Congratulations! You just pampered yourself with twenty-one-days of amazingly delicious raw food. E-mail me and tell me about it: junelouks@verizon.net.

Chapter Sixteen: Kitchen Equipment

Blender: Essential. There are lots of blenders out there, but, in my experience, none compare to the Vita-Mix 3 (professional line—$500); It blends smoothies in seconds. Within 1-2 minutes in the blender, mylks and soups get nice and warm. See Blenderpros.com (800-422-7980) for a sound abatement cover ($159) or check out their latest Vitamix, the Advanced In Counter Blending Station with attached sound abatement cover ($879). Higher priced, but it beats the price of an oven.

Soybella: Makes fresh almond mylk (as well as other mylks from nuts and seeds) in 30 seconds! Available at tribestlife.com

Dehydrator: Fresh fruit and veggies are always my first choice for more hydrating meals, but ahh … the smell of fresh raw cookies from the dehydrator! With a dehydrator, raw food rises to a new level. When food is dried, it can be stored easily. Although more work, dehydrated food makes the transition from cooked to living food easier. When the temperature of the food goes above 95 degrees, it starts dying, and when it rises above 118 degrees, it is dead (you can't plant it anymore).

Before we owned a dehydrator, we put the food in the warming drawer, but that didn't work because warming drawers retain the moisture. Then we tried putting the food in the sun, protecting it from flies and birds with a cheese cloth. Summer sun works great, perhaps even better than a dehydrator, as long as you can keep an eye out for approaching shade. In the winter, you can put your oven on the lowest setting and leave the drawer open, but not if small children are in reach.

Now, I have a 5-tray Excalibur dehydrator I bought online and a stainless steel Sausage Maker dehydrator I purchased from Don Kidson's local "Busy Bee" Hardware Store. The Sausage Maker cost $200 more than the Excalibur (at $199) but it not only looks nicer in the kitchen, it holds 10 trays and doesn't have the hum like the black plastic Excalibur. Also, some ovens, like the Wolf Electric Stove Top Oven, have a dehydrating feature. Finally, sproutman.com has a great new dehydrator that you can add trays to as your family's needs grow, the Sproutman 4 Tray Dehydrator, $149.

When foods are moist, I set the temperature at 145 degrees (the moisture keeps the actual temperature of the food at around 95 degrees.) As the food dries, I drop the temp to 105 or 100 degrees.

An endless list of plant food dehydrates well. Dehydrate fruits and veggies, crackers and cookies, nuts and seeds. We sometimes dehydrate coconut, as most store-bought shredded coconut is pasteurized. (Sun Organic Farm has dehydrated coconut.) Leftover fruits and veggies dehydrate well. Enjoy the crunch! If you purchase dried foods, make sure they don't contain sulfur or chemical preservatives.

Teflex Sheets: These sheets have a durable, nonstick, nonporous surface and are usually available as an option when purchasing a dehydrator (which always comes with mesh sheets). I place the Teflex sheets on top of the mesh sheets when I have gooey mixtures that would otherwise seep through the mesh. (Available from Don Kidson, Busy Bee Hardware, Santa Monica, CA.)

Food Processor: Using it will save you lots of *time*. We use a Cuisinart.

Juicer: Optional in my book because a juicer removes important fiber, and juicers are expensive. Wheatgrass gets too hot with the Champion juicer, so nutrients are lost. I recommend the Twin Gear juicer. It not only keeps the juice at a mild temperature, it also has a blank plate. With the blank plate, you can mix sprouted grains and frozen ice cream easily.

For the "Lemonaid" and "Orange Juice Popsicles," I recommend a citrus juicer or a citrus press. It's a good tool for separating the seeds from the fruit for the smoothies. Blended citrus seeds not only taste bad, some citrus seeds have toxins in them.

I have never juiced much myself. The children love to juice citrus. I have taught them all how to use the citrus juicer, and the eldest sister will cut the oranges in half. It is an activity they all enjoy.

Ice-Cream Maker: Not essential, but homemade ice cream is hard to beat, and it is fun for the kids. I think the most important factor in choosing an ice-cream maker is the type of metal used for its bowl. If we must have metal touch our food, stainless steel has been determined to be the most stable. In the past, we used the inexpensive "Krups" ($30), but the canister is aluminum. That was before my blood test came back high in aluminum. (The Cuisinart Ice Cream Makers are also aluminum, as well as the Kitchen-Aid Mixer Attachment). So out it goes—I don't want metals in general touching the food, especially aluminum. Lehmans (Lehmans.com) has a good, old-fashioned ice-cream maker with a stainless-steel canister that cools mechanically when surrounded in ice and rock salt. The blade, however, is not stainless steel.

After an exhaustive search, I found a website that offers several types of non-aluminum ice cream makers that range from $69 to $999, depending on how many you plan to feed these delicious recipes to. Go to www.1-800-espresso.com. I tried the $109 Dolce Vita Electric model, but the ice cream didn't freeze. Then at the time of this printing upgraded to the $279 Gelato "Chef 2200"... and hopefully we will find success! I am determined to find an effective stainless steel ice cream maker!

If you don't have an ice cream maker, mix the freezing liquid in a glass bowl every 10 minutes while it freezes, or, even better, put the frozen mixture through the twin-gear juicer (using the blank plate).

Again, my only hesitation with ice-cream makers is the metal bowl and blade. Avoid aluminum; make sure it is stainless steel. In general, keep your food away from metal surfaces as much as possible.

The Ultimate Knife: If you are chopping a lot like me, you might appreciate buying a ceramic knife. I recommend Kyocera or Choisons Ceramic Cutlery. They not only stay sharp up to 10 times longer than stainless steel, they don't react with foods, keeping your food looking and tasting fresher, longer. The drawback is they need to be sent out to be sharpened. Since I started using one, I no longer use our stainless-steel knives.

To save chopping time, put several vegetables under the blade at the same time, and use a chef's knife. Also, in regards to slicing the linguini, if you use a mandolin, it's quick and easy. And my favorite, for angel hair pasta, is the Saladacco.

Cutting Board: Nontreated bamboo is ideal; I'm still attached to my polypropylene (plastic) board. These boards are less porous than wood, making it less likely to harbor bacteria and easier to clean. If you use wood, always chop onion and garlic (alliums) on a separate board. Regardless, have separate boards if you have meat or dairy in your kitchen. (See cleaning recipes for an easy way to clean and freshen up your boards, and clean them often.)

Microwave: Throw it away!

Chapter Seventeen: Sprouting

I'm told failure always comes before success. When it comes to growing beautiful three-inch sprouts in the kitchen, I have ... utterly failed. Anything I try to grow over two days becomes a moldy, putrid disaster area, even when armed with a bottle of food grade hydrogen peroxide spray. Then, I have made the mistake of putting the putrid mess in our composter, making a humongous putrid mess. Perhaps that is why I have put off writing this chapter until last.

I trust success will come. There is a recognized sprout guru in the raw food world, Steve Meyerowitz, also known as "Sproutman" (Go to Sproutman.com). No doubt I should have started with him at the get-go. It is on my list of future projects.

However, germinating is *easy*, and for the purpose of this book, that is all you will need to learn to do.

Here's the basic recipe:

— Soak the seeds or nuts in water for the prescribed time included in the recipe. (You can buy a sprouting jar for this or use a glass bowl; just avoid using anything with metal.) Some nuts can absorb half of its water, so be sure to leave room for extra water at the top. Soaking is necessary to release the enzyme inhibitors that make the seed or nut difficult to digest.

— At the prescribed time, toss the water but don't toss the babies out with it. If you don't have a sprout jar, use a loose-pile cheesecloth (or nonmetal strainer), pouring out the water while firmly holding the cheesecloth around the rim of the bowl. Fill bowl with water again and repeat several times, rinsing the babies thoroughly. The water may be colored. Those are the enzyme inhibitors. Rinse until there is no more color to the water.

— After soaking, the nuts (and flaxseeds) are germinated and ready to eat or go into a recipe. The seeds are ready for sprouting. Cover seeds with a dry cheesecloth and tuck away into a dark place if possible. If the sprouting time is more than a day, be sure to rinse the sprouts daily.

— At the prescribed time, or before, either add the sprouts to your recipe or refrigerate. Refrigeration will slow down the sprouting. Use within three days of refrigeration.

We buy our clover sprouts and pea sprouts at the local co-op. Because of the very slim chance of E. coli and Salmonella (the risk is much higher with meat and dairy), all sprout growers wash their sprouts with chlorine. This negative far outweighs the positives. What was that Web site? (sproutman.com)

Chapter Eighteen:
A Recipe for Water

Divide your body weight by two. This is the number of ounces of pure water to drink each day (usually eight to twelve eight-ounce glasses for adults). Juice, coffee, tea, and smoothies don't count as pure water.

Drink water especially first thing in the morning and before bedtime. Avoid drinking half an hour before a meal or one and a half hours after a meal.

What is the best water to drink? The 1940s ushered in the practice of adding chlorine (and fluoride) to public-water systems; we drink it and our children are breathing the chlorine stream in their showers daily. Many of us use filters, removing the chlorine and a host of other toxic chemicals, but also striping the water of its natural minerals.

My friend Don Kidson refers to bottled water as bacteria in a bottle. I have found water that has been in a glass *tastes* much better than water that has been sitting in plastic. Major bottled-water companies in the U.S. filter and bottle water from city water, even The Bronx of New York (look for the fine print on the bottle that says PWS [public water supply].)

I suggest installing *a filter, a whole-house filter* if you can, and having another gratitude system for loving your drinking water. We have Roxtract Water (see roxtract.net). This is a system that adds minerals back into the water with reverse osmosis and sits in our kitchen in a big, blue, glass container, giving it a chance to re-structure with negative ions, so the molecules of the water are smaller and more easily absorbed during digestion. Letting the water sit for a few days also gives the water an opportunity to adjust to our space of gratitude and love.

My friend Don has been led to distill his water. He suggests getting a small house distiller which gently removes chlorine and chemicals. Also, at Sproutman's Web site (sproutman.com), he suggests a filtering system that ionizes water.

Not being an authority on water (and even if there is an authority), I suggest thinking this through for yourself, and coming up with what is best for your individual family. As much as possible, avoid drinking water in plastic bottles. Use glass containers for your water when you are on the road and stainless steel containers for the kids and sports activities. Keep water by your side and enjoy water often.

Water Experiment:

The smaller the water molecules, the more easily the water can be absorbed by the intestines. Test out the size of the molecules of the various samples of water, by observing how quickly the water is absorbed by the wood:

    1 piece of Untreated Wood
    1/8 t Tap Water
    1/8 t Filtered Water
    1/8 t Distilled Water
    1/8 t "Loved" Water
    1/8 t "Hated" Water

Come up with your own version of loved and hated water. Perhaps it is the way you speak to it or printed words you show it. Pour each water sample on the wood, six inches apart. The race is on! Note which water sample is absorbed by the wood most quickly.

Note: most cutting boards have some kind of finish or oil rubbed on them. Be sure to use a raw piece of wood.

Chapter Nineteen: A Recipe for Health

1. A good night's sleep

2. Breathe fresh, clean air, deeply

3. Drink pure water (eight to twelve glasses for adults)

4. Sunshine

5. Rawumptious Diet (fresh, hydrating, mineral-rich plant food)

6. Laughter

7. Exercise

8. Follow your calling

9. Love; someone to love; connection

10. Spiritual discipline; path with prayer; mediation

Indulge in all ingredients, daily.

Chapter Twenty:
Chemical-Free, Often Organic Cosmetics and Sunscreens

Cruelty free and vegan

This is only a partial list. I include this because, since leaving my chemical-laden cosmetic company, I have been scouring the shelves of spas, health-food stores, and direct-selling companies looking for better options. I have purchased many products, only to find hidden chemical preservatives, other toxic ingredients, or the products simply weren't that great. So I offer this to you as some good alternatives, but I am surely leaving out others. For an extensive list, go to cosmeticdatabase.com. This Web site (Skin Deep) is a safety guide to cosmetics and personal-care products, written by researchers at the Environmental Working Group, *"because the FDA doesn't require companies to test their own products for safety."* Another great Web site for purchasing cosmetics is rejuvinateorganics.com.

Thirteen Body-Care Toxins to Avoid:

1. Mercury: also avoid the mercury preservative "thimerosal"
2. Lead: listed as "lead acetate"
3. Nanoparticles
4. Placenta
5. Hydroquinone skin lightener
6. Phthalates
7. Petroleum byproducts (mineral oil, 1,4-dioxane)
8. Fragrance
9. Parabens
10. Active Ingredients
11. Formaldehyde
12. Toulene
13. Coal Tar
(adapted from coopamerica.org)

A basic, wonderful staple for dry skin is fresh-pressed flaxseed oil, and it is a healthy oil for our body to drink up. Avocado oil, coconut oil, and many other natural oils work great too, mixed with a few teaspoons of your favorite essential oils. Fresh avocado is a delicious mask for dry skin, while cucumber smoothed over the skin is refreshing for oilier- to combination-skin types.

Eucalyptus oil is my favorite essential oil to put in the bath. You just have to try it. Essential oils are a wonderful aromatherapy but are too strong to be applied directly on the skin.

Sunscreens: In my opinion, most importantly, we want to be sure to avoid putting chemical and medicated sunscreens on our children and ourselves. Shea butter has a natural sunscreen, if you are looking for a simple oil for short exposures. For longer exposures, go for the SPF 30s:

*UV Natural Sport 30 Broad Spectrum Sunscreen: June's favorite; very water resistant, even after eighty minutes of surfing. The only active ingredient is Zinc Oxide (however it doesn't make your skin white). This has natural oils in it (which feel great, not greasy), so it is probably best for normal to dry skin types.

Holistic Enterprises Sunscreen SPF 30: Check it out—no chemicals, no active ingredients, and feels wonderful on your skin! Not waterproof.

Dr. Hauschka SPF 30 Sunscreen Cream for Children and Sensitive Skin: Very water resistant (works for us surfers most triumphantly!), but leaves a white cast to the skin.

*Aubrey Organics: The children like it; UVA/UVB protection; active ingredients: Padimate O (PABA Ester) and Titanium Dioxide; not waterproof. (Note of warning: some people are highly allergic Padimate O.)

California Baby SPF 30 Plus Sunscreen: Very water resistant and Jeff's favorite sunscreen. During the summer, the "natural bug blend" helps to retard bees and mosquitoes. Gives a white cast to the skin.

Jason's Sunscreens

Facial Care:
MSN by Ultra Aesthetics: My favorite. Light, great for all skin types, smells good, wonderful moisturizers.

Earthscience: Fragrance free, great for oily and combination skin.

*Mychelle: Has wonderful moisturizers and a great gentle exfoliator with fruit enzymes.

Astara Biogenic Skin Care: Great daily refining scrub

*Juice Beauty: Ninety-five percent organic and great for all skin types. This would be my favorite line of facial care, except that they use xanthan gum, a highly processed derivative from corn (not natural). Like many products used in the cosmetic industry, xanthan gum has not been assessed for safety in the cosmetics industry. I include it because I admire the company's commitment to using organic ingredients. Their mask exfoliates with a fruit acid. They have a creamy cleanser, excellent moisturizer, and wonderful eye and lip treatments. Although, again, do I want my children or myself eating xanthan gum? They also have a lower-priced brand, Juice Organics. Juice Organic formulations are less concentrated and use about five organic juices instead of twenty-six juices, but they are still a nice product (and affordable!) ... and mostly organic.

Facial Care and Make-up:

Dr Hauschka: I liked everything in this line. (Except for the mascara; it irritated my eyes.) Moisturizing Mask is great for those dry days. The lip glosses do not have any mineral oils or preservatives or chemical colors or dyes. Just think about how many pounds of lipstick women digest in their lifetimes. With all the chemical lip glosses we had as a family, including the girl's "play" lip glosses (is that glitter in there?), we had a toxic waste cleanup session. Get rid of it.

*Iredale Mineral cosmetics: Formulated for cancer patients. Overall, a nice line. Great mascara. I didn't try the skin care.

Dr Janet Zand: Facial moisturizer and correcting eye serum are light and hydrating. Love it!

Body Care:

I have been on a quest to find a good body scrub. My skin is too sensitive for body brushing or loofahs. They feel like brillo. I think body scrubbing is stimulating and helps to remove toxins and dead layers of skin. I highly recommend it. My favorite scrubs are fine salt and fresh pressed flaxseed oil or blended pumpkin with flaxseed oil, straight from the kitchen! (Blended apple or blackberry with avocado, coconut oil and flaxseed oil are also wonderful.)

*Dr. Bronners Magic Soaps: Eucalyptus is my favorite. Soap bars for the body as well as liquid cleansers for the kitchen (and body). Good-bye Palmolive! (This company uses certified, organic, olive oil from Palestinian farmers occupied on the West Bank, who tend one-thousand-year-old orchards that have never been sprayed with pesticides, and workers of an Israeli kibbutz.

Pagea Organics: soap bars.

Blooming Lotus: soap bars.

Epicuren: Wonderful! Expensive, but wonderful, especially the Rosemary Body Lotion and Body Scrub. Epicuren's key ingredients come from the rainforests, which on one hand supports the environment by making the rainforests economically viable. However, Epicuren's Web site isn't clear about the sustainability of their farming practices. Great lip balms and facial skin care as well.

*Avalon Organics: Great Rosemary Hand and Body Lotion, fairly priced.

Aura-Cacia: Incredible, oil-based Grapefruit-Tangerine Body Scrub for the shower. Stimulating, invigorating scent.

*Aubrey Organics: Invigorating Body Polish leaves skin silky and smooth; great for the shower. Also has a great shampoo.

Aroma Therapeutics: Mental Clarity Rosemary and Lemongrass Natural Body Scrub. Wow! It is fairly light on the oils, so it's great in the tub.

Karite-One Pure Shea Butter: Great for super-dry skin or chapped areas. Smooth onto damp skin. Shea butter is a natural sunscreen.

Hugo: Quality ingredients, nice products.

MSM: **This entire line is great, especially the body scrub for the bath.**

100% Pure: Great body scrub! puritycosmetics.com.

Hair Care:
Kiss My Face: "Obsessively Organic" Shampoos and conditioners.
MSM Ultra Aesthetics Hair Care: No lauryl sulfites or sulfates.
Intelligent Nutrients: Applies rigorous organic and fair-trade standards to all the ingredients in the hair-care (and body-care) products.
EO: Shampoos and conditioners; great scents.

Dental Care:
*Jason's Natural Products: Finally a toothpaste without lauryl sulfates that the kids like. Powersmile is our favorite.
Dental Herb Company: A great mouthwash without alcohol or artificial sweeteners, "The Tonic."

*Active supporters of either/or both: the Compact for Global Production of Safer Health and Beauty Products and the Safe Cosmetics Campaign.

Chapter Twenty-one:
A Raw Gardener's Wish List

In case this book leaves you inspired to plant a vegetable garden, here is my list of favorites:

Fall: sweet peas, chard, collards, garlic (with the roses), onions, other leafy greens; beans and peas for cover crops

Winter: lettuce, onions, parsley, kohlrabi, kale and other cold hardy leafy greens.

Spring: spinach (with strawberries), cabbage (with mint, thyme and chamomile), chard, comfrey, lettuce

Mid spring: heirloom tomatoes with celery, parsley and basil, peppers, hot peppers, melons, cucumbers, watermelons, zucchini, squash

Summer: broccoli, summer lettuce, corn, and cucumbers with sunflowers, squash, beets, basil, zucchini

Fruit trees: avocado, loquat, plum, peach, nectarine, apple, mulberry, pomegranate, sapote, cherimoya, guava, apricot, banana (tree and plant), mango, papaya, and citrus (Navel, Valencia, Cara Cara, and Blood oranges; Improved Meyer lemon, Meyer lime, Tahitian lime, grapefruit, cumquat)

In separate beds: artichoke; asparagus (and with tomato, parsley, and basil);raspberries with garlic; blackberries; blueberries; strawberries; Goji berries; horseradish around plum trees; tansy, nasturtiums, and chives around fruit trees; onions to defend against ants; lemon balm and lemon grass; watercress in greenhouse; stinging nettles; ginger/wild ginger; turmeric and evening primrose; potatoes (for the children)

And I am sure there are other delicious greens. Pea and flax make good cover crops. Go to turtletreeseeds.com for biodynamic and organic seeds, and treesofantiquity.com for organic fruit trees and rootstock.

Smiles

Conclusion

When I decided I wanted to feed my family delicious, living, plant-based foods, I was charting new territory. The recipes I had in my raw books were not kid tested. If you were looking for recipes your whole family will love, hopefully you found them here.

I also hope this book inspires you to take your own adventure toward greater health for yourself, your family, and our planet's sustainability. Your journey may start with food, but it soon becomes clear that everything is connected and spiritual. Our food choices stem from our spiritual direction, are often emotional, and strengthened or undermined by our focus. Spirituality connects us all and weaves through every layer of our lives. We are linked in so many ways, and our children model what we do. As role models, it is time to examine what we are advertising and promoting. When I hear adults complain about eating plant foods, it's no wonder that their children won't eat them either. When we take a stand to make healthy choices, we are also guiding our children. This guidance gives them the inspiration and strength to follow suit. This strength and inspiration is ultimately spiritual.

I hope you share these recipes with your children, family, and friends, and remember that sometimes we need to try a new food ten times before we like it. Our family experience has shown that when the whole family plants, prepares, and harvests the food, they will want to own it. As a result, they eat much more of a plant-based diet than ever before.

I hope this book has been a bridge for you to delve deeper into your own experience of Source, prompting you to take your health into your own hands, strengthen your immune system, reduce inflammation, and get your organs into optimum efficiency; becoming what your Maker always intended for you as radiant, vibrant, energetic, and balanced.

I hope you see that this physical self is the spiritual self in visible form. If we want to change this physical self, the place to start is with surrender to that higher power that is guiding and present in all of us and our decisions. Listen to it.

And I hope this book will be a source of ideas for some of your own, inspired, delicious, *Rawumptious* recipes.

Blessings to the new, beautiful you.

June Louks

Acknowledgments

Most importantly, we would like to acknowledge Olga Amaya for her tireless, enthusiastic, and creative assistance in our kitchen. Olga's contributions and ideas are weaved throughout this book. Our recipes have been perfected by her repeated use of them, and when Mama Louks was busy writing, researching, and gathering ideas for this book, our family has enjoyed these recipes many times over because of Olga.

"Yummy French Toast" and "Coconut Brownie Balls" were inspired by *Raw Food/Real World* by Matthew Kenney and Sarma Melngailis. "Vegan Tuna" was inspired from RAWvolution, by Matt Amsden. "Caesar Salad Dressing" and "Chocolate Chip Cookies" were inspired from Charlie Trotter and Roxanne Klein's "Raw" Recipe book. "Green Soup" was inspired by Anna Anawalt.

"Easy Banana Ice Cream" was contributed by girlfriend Lisa Cooper. Brigitte Robindore, thank you for your pesto recipe. Lisa and Brigitte are both inspirations for me as they provide healthy vegetarian meals for their family.

"McMillan Dressing" was contributed by the raw McMillan/Von Hagen Family.

"Carob Balls," "Mint Chocolate Chip Cookies" and "Carmel Chew" were created by my girlfriend Nanette Bercu because "I love cookies!" Finally, "Coconut Yogurt" was inspired by Don Kidson, who is known by some as the "Hardware Humanitarian" and by others as the "Juice Prophet"; going on twenty years raw.

And a big thanks you to the great and talented: Martha Quinn, Deborah Kramer, Aunt Mary, Debra Louks, and Linda McCann for reviewing the book with a fine-toothed comb.

Appendix

A letter to our local public school to address junk food policies at school

Before I share my letter with you, I'm going to share a letter from a fellow mom that illustrates the frustration with schools that don't have a good junk food policy:

"I'm probably going to call/write administrators at LAUSD. I feel like to truly make a change I need to reach 'higher.' After talking 1:1 with _____ after the meeting, I got the impression that *if* any changes were made at all, they would be slow and incremental. It doesn't seem 'right' that a public school should be allowed to continue to 'poison' our children.

"Just yesterday, while I was waiting for David (my fourth grader) at pick up, I was talking to Benjamin's (my kindergartner) room parent about your forthcoming letter. And David came over to me eating from a bag of candy he got in his classroom for Chinese New Year. Then, we walked by the Krispy Kreme doughnut table on our way out of the main entrance. Of course, Benjamin was whining and complaining that it wasn't fair that he didn't get candy like his brother and wanted some. Then, it was on to the Krispy Kreme 'fight.' It shouldn't be like this at our school.

"I look forward to hearing more of your thoughts and ideas" (Nancy, Pacific Palisades)

February 14, 2007

Dear Principal Hollis and Governing Board of Marquez School,

This letter is to encourage you to rewrite your policies and ban unhealthy snacks.

Eighteen percent of our children are obese (18 percent and climbing. See attachment, front page of the *Los Angeles Times*, September 2006) and 5 percent of (our children!) are diabetic. Kid's today have weaker bones and arm fractures are up 42 percent from 1970. Isn't it time we made some changes to our food policy? All of these health challenges are diet related (to junk food), yet as a school we continue with Krispy Kreme sales because the school makes *money*? This is short-term (financial) gain for a long-term sacrifice (our children's health). Is it really worth it? What about the fruit of the week from the farmer's market? Those Satsuma Tangerines or Arkansas Apples out right now are delicious! Instead, we have lemonade and bake sales, and then sugary, white, floury foods in the classroom for holidays, birthday parties, and then junk food to celebrate hard work or even junk food just for fun. Friday, one of my daughters had just come from another junk food just for fun (just Vanilla Wafers) party in the classroom. What about reading a short story? What about orange or apple slices? What about stickers? At the September, three-day Fifth Grade Big Bear Retreat, this white stuff was the most highly promoted and consumed "food" (a.k.a. junk food) group. Our first-grade booth at the Halloween Festival was filling sand candy in vials for the children to eat.

Sugar is addictive, and as a school we (as parents, teachers, and as a community) are encouraging our children's sugar addictions. White sugar weakens our immune system. Although my fifth graders can now make more discerning choices about their food, my first grader can't even spell "diabetic," let alone understand what it means. Yet, weekly, they are forced to make another junk-food choice.

The bottom line is that white sugar and white flour have zero fiber or natural nutrients. These simple carbohydrates (as well as juice and soda), leach minerals (calcium) from our teeth and bones. They are not foods, but junk foods.

Apples, pears, tangerines, pumpkin, and sunflower seeds (the list of these often neglected, plant-based foods that children enjoy is long, and we'd be happy to offer more ideas in this area) are popular with the kids, too, but they don't sell if they are competing with sugar. We need to stop promoting junk food at our schools!

Please, please stop allowing white sugar and white flour in the classroom. Please put an end to junk-food parties and sales in our precious school!

Sincerely,

June and Jeff Louks

Recommended Reading

General:

365 Ways to Save the Earth by Philippe Bourseiller (our friends have this in their powder room—what a great idea!)

Raw Family by the Boutenko Family, Raw Family Publishing, 2000

Green for Life, by Victoria Boutenko, Raw Family Publishing, 2005 (I also recommend her CD "Greens Can Save Your Life")

Edible and Useful Plants of California by Charlotte Bringle Clarke, University of California Press, 1977

The China Study by T. Colin Campbell, Ph.D. and Thomas M Campbell II, Benbella Books, 2005

Force of Nature, by Laird Hamilton, Rodale Publishers, 2008 (Laird, as a role model of super-human surfing excellence, inspires us, as parents and kids, to stay away from processed foods and exercise often)

Rainbow Green Live-Food Cuisine, by Gabriel Cousens, MD, North Atlantic Books, 2003, as well as *Spiritual Nutrition*, Gabriel Cousens, MD, 2005)

Sugar Blues by William Dufty, Warner Books, 1975

The Hidden Messages from Water, Masaru Emoto and David A Thayne

Animal, Vegetable, Miracle by Barbara Kingsolver, Harper Collins Publishers, 2007 (A story of her family's attempt at being "locavores," eating better and offering a strategy to save the planet ... the inexpensive joy of life as a locavore.) Kingsolver's novel, *Prodigal Summer* is an entertaining read, and also an education on biology, the food chain, and conventional versus organic farming. "... countless intimate lessons of biology, the realities of small farming, and the final, urgent truth that humans are only one part of life on earth."

Sweetness and Power by Sidney W. Mintz, The Place of Sugar in Modern History

Whole Foods Companion, by Diane Onstad, Chelsea Green Publishing Company, 2004

Diet for a New America: How Your Food Choices Affect Your Health, Happiness, and the Future of Life on Earth by John Robbins (son of founder of Baskin Robbins), Stillpoint, 1987

Raw Kids by Cheryl Stoycoff, Living Spirit Press, 2004

The Sunfood Diet Success System by David Wolfe, Maul Brothers Publishing, 2006

Naked Chocolate by David Wolfe and Shazzie, Maul Brothers Publishing, 2005

Eating, a DVD by Michael Anderson (This DVD converted our family to a vegetarian lifestyle.)

The Cove, directed by Fisher Stevens (A documentary about the dolphin slaughter in Taiji, Japan which converted a girlfriend to be a vegetarian.)

The Omnivore's Dilemma—A Natural History of Four Meals by Michael Pollan (note: Although Michael Pollan's book is a great read, and his description of our "National

Eating Disorder" eye opening, there is no "dilemma." Nutrient rich foods are available in the plant world.)

Too Much of a Good Thing: Raising Children of Character in an Indulgent Age by Dan Kindling, PhD (note: this is the only book here I haven't read. The title has nothing to do with raw food, and at the same time, everything to do with it)

The 80/10/10 Diet by Douglas Graham, FoodnSport Press, 2006

Skinny Bitch by Rory Freedman and Kim Barnovin (not children's lit ... offensive language, but motivating and informative about sugar, carnivores, dairy products, meat and industry, cheese, and all the lousy ingredients that go into our processed foods.)

Your Body's Many Cries For Water (You Are Not Sick You Are Thirsty! Don't Treat Thirst with Medications!), F. Batmanghelidj, M.D., Global Health Solutions, Inc., 2006. (Batmanghelidj also shares how salt is essential yet fails to share that organic salt (through organic celery, greens, tomatoes, etc.) is healthier than inorganic sea salt.)

Recipe Books:

Eat Smart, Eat Raw by Kate Wood, Square One Publishers, 2006

Raw Food Real World by Matthew Kenney and Sara Bengalis, Regan Books, 2005

RAWvolution by Matt Amsden, Regan, 2006

Rainbow Green Live Food Cuisine by Dr. Gabriel Cousens

Rawsome!: Maximizing Health, Energy, and Culinary Delight with the Raw Foods Diet by Brigitte Mars

Raw Food Life Force Energy by Natalia Rose (a good transitioning book)

Raw by Charlie Trotter and Roxanne Klein, Ten Speed Press, 2003

Vegan Fusion World Cuisine by Mark Reinfeld and Bo Rinaldi, Beaufortbooks, 2007

Gardening Books:

Earth User's Guide To Permaculture by Rosemary Morrow, Kangaroo Press, 2006

Gaia's Garden (A guide to Home-Scale Permaculture) by Toby Hemenway, Chelsea Green Publishing Company, 2000

Children's Books:

Herb, The Vegetarian Dragon by Julie Bass and Debbie Harter

Play with Your Food by Joust Offers and Saxton Freeman (and his other books for children)

Old Turtle and the Broken Truth by Douglas Wood

The Lorax by Dr. Seuss

Whole World (book and CD) by Fred Penne and Christopher Carr

The Secret of Water by Masaru Emoto, Atria Books, 2006

Index